3 SKIPS AND A JUMP

to Becoming a
WOMAN OF INFLUENCE

TAMMY HOTSENPILLER

3 Skips and a Jump to Becoming a Woman of Influence
All rights reserved.

Published by Total Life Coach
Copyright © 2015 by Tammy Hotsenpiller
Cover Design by Simone Gabryk
Book Design and Production by Simone Gabryk
Photography: James Davis II
Editing by Joy Bancroft

First Printing: December 2014
Second Printing: August 2017
Printed in the United States of America
First Edition: December 2014
Second Edition: August 2017

FOREWORD

Once you start reading this book, it will take you on a journey to clean up your heart. Setting a pattern to get rid of negative thought processes is so freeing, and that is exactly what you are going to find here. It is a clear and detailed path to find your way to wholeness.

Tammy's engaging style and her heart to explain negative emotions that hit us all is huge. Her stories intertwined with practical advice resonate and reveal what is holding you back from being the Woman of Influence God has created you to be. Once these emotional roadblocks are unearthed and revealed, she provides practical answers on how to create a whole new way of thinking and looking at your life. Tammy takes you down the road to liberty, showing you how to plough through obstacles swiftly and surely. Enjoy and savor each chapter in this life-changing guide, knowing that a journey of a thousand miles begins with one step. If you are looking for emotional freedom, you have come to the right place.

Mary Hudson
Arise International

ACKNOWLEDGMENTS

Thank you to the TLC team who made this book a reality. I could not have done it without you. Your relentless love and patience have made me the woman I am today. Marlene Tafoya, Sheree Petersen, and Lisa Haines are truly examples of Women of Influence. You will forever be at the center of my heart. I love each of you dearly.

To all the Women of Influence in Anaheim Hills, California, who have stood by my side and made me the leader I am today: Thank you. Your faith and encouragement have kept me going when I have needed it most. The Women of Influence NEW Conference challenged all of us to ask ourselves: What NEW thing does God have for me? Writing this book was on the list for me.

To my daughter Jen Hotsenpiller Ramlet. Thank you for allowing me to practice all my mentorship principles on you. The NEW Women's Conference was your launching pad, and you have touched countless lives with your story. You truly are a Woman of Influence.

To my sweet LA friends who not only endorsed this book but also shared their stories of Influence: Thank you for touching countless lives for the kingdom.

Caitlin Crosby Benward, Heidi Tuttle, Virginia Morse Kramer, Allison Trowbridge, Ashley Allen, Kristin Dalton Wolfe, Christa Black Gifford, Tiffany Dupont

To Mary Hudson who told me I must write a book that would speak to women's hearts: You are a dear friend and role model for me. Thank you for loving Jesus and letting your light shine.

To Michelle Patterson and Tina Konkin, two Orange County Women of Influence: The California Women's Conference and Relationship Help Centers have been powerful platforms for me to personally affiliate with. Your vision and inspiration have shaped the lives of many women around the globe.

Thank you to my wonderful friends who helped edit and critique this manuscript. Your confidence keeps me moving forward. Donna Guiles, Rosalie Puleo, and Lori DeAngelo, I love you. To my editor, Joy Bancroft: Thank you for sharing your time, talent, and passion with me to make this book a reality. You are truly a Woman of Influence in my life. To my layout editor and book designer, Jill Burch: Thank you for the creativity and time you invested in this book; you have been a great blessing to the project.

To my best friend and gracious husband, Phil Hotsenpiller: Not only did you encourage me through affirmation and prayer, but you also provided humor along the way. You saw something in me before I saw it in myself. You are the best definition of Influence I know. May God continue to use you to impact the hearts and lives of everyone who crosses your path. You are a blessing to mankind.

To my wonderful kids: You are the lifeblood of my heart. You have helped form me into the woman I am today. Your lives have touched the very core of my being. I pray I will always be a Woman of Influence in your lives. Thank you for all my wonderful grandchildren. I am a blessed woman.

To every woman brave enough to read this book: May the pages inspire and equip you to become the Woman of Influence God created you to be. May you see His glorious plan for your life as you read the stories of Influence found in this book.

WE are on our way to

BECOMING the WOMEN

GOD sees us to be.

ENDORSEMENTS

Tammy Hotsenpiller is truly a Woman of Influence. Having personally worked with her on the California Women's Conference, I know her commitment to see women equipped and empowered to become all they were created to be. Tammy's gift as a Life Coach has impacted lives around the world. *3 Skips and a Jump* will take you where you desire to be!

Michelle Patterson
President of the California Women's Conference and CEO of Women Network

Tammy Hotsenpiller is creative, passionate, energetic, and highly motivational. Her workshops on life balance and on professional and personal development are truly inspiring and life changing! She is truly a Woman of Influence.

Christine Sakdalan
Vice President, Diabetes Marketing, Patient Centric Strategy and Solutions

This book is absolutely revelational. I learned about the power of putting away all excuses so I could jump into my destiny. Tammy has stories to draw from and has the ability to speak to women from all walks of life. When I read this book, I felt like it was written just for me. You will be a powerful, influential, confident woman when you are finished with this life-changing book.

Kristen Dalton
2009 Miss USA, Founder & Writer, SheIsMore.com

It's difficult to put into words the incredible impact Tammy has had on my life. The most crucial lesson I have learned from Tammy is the importance of incorporating balance and rest into my daily life—a woman who is run ragged is of little help to anyone. However, a balanced, rested woman, who functions from a place of peace, rather than a place of chaos, can truly help and influence many.

Ashley Allen
Wife, Mother, Producer (The Bachelor, Hell's Kitchen, America's Got Talent)

Tammy Hotsenpiller is one of the strongest and most inspirational women I've ever known. She practices what she preaches.

Caitlin Crosby
Singer, Songwriter, & Actress

Tammy has sown so much into my life with personal mentorship, life coaching, and friendship. The wisdom, honor, respect, and sacrifice that she pours into other people is beautiful. She has already changed the world, and I would read anything she writes and give it to everyone whom I cared about because if it makes us garner the wisdom to have the qualities that she has... then we are WINNING.

Heidi Tuttle
Director of Acquisitions, Truli Media Group
Casting Director (MTV, VH1, BET, CBS/Paramount, NBC, Bravo, Lifetime, & WB)

Tammy has been a coach, friend, and influence in my life, as well as a mom, wife, and leader in the lives of others. She has the insight and compassion to influence women to go to the next level—a healthy level. I hope, as women, we will let this book and Tammy's insight take us to the next level—physically, emotionally, and spiritually. As a relationship counselor and conference speaker, I would recommend you consider becoming an influence in your world.

Tina Konkin
Owner, Marriage & Help Centers, Orange County, CA

Tammy's ability to coach and encourage is truly a gift from God. She has encouraged me through the years to not only follow my dreams but also to dream bigger. Through wisdom and experience she inspires women to rise up into their true identity and to be all that they are created to be! I know this book will encourage women and change lives across the nations.

Virginia Morse Kramer
Model & Speaker

Tammy has been more than a life coach to me. She has stretched me in ways I never thought were possible. I never could have been confident enough to use the gifts God gave me or become an inspiration to others without the coaching and cheering on from Tammy. I can honestly say I would not be the woman that I am becoming if I hadn't met Tammy Hotsenpiller.

Kim Vinson
Owner CEO Kimmie's Coffee Cup
Voted Best Breakfast Restaurant in Orange County, CA

Tammy is a spiritual warrior with the heart of a mother, the wisdom of a·sage, and the loving ear of your best friend. She is driven by a consuming passion to build up the spiritual, mental, and emotional health of the next generation, and she does so with enthusiasm, compassion, whimsy, and grace. Savor these words: They are from a new mentor who wants to see you thrive!

Allison Trowbridge
President, Copper Pictures
Partner, Just Business

There are only two types of people in this world—those who are influenced by their surroundings, and those who influence the surrounding around them. In *3 Skips and a Jump*, Tammy Hotsenpiller puts a treasure chest of practical tools within our hands, coaching each reader into their fullest potential!

Christa Black Gifford
Author, speaker, multi-platinum selling songwriter

TABLE OF CONTENTS

INTRODUCTION

The title for this book was inspired by a coaching session that's a real example of what happens when we allow our emotions and excuses to cripple us, when we fail to see the gifts and opportunities God has intended for us.

It was a sunny spring morning the day I met with Emilee. I had determined it would be my last coaching session with her if something did not change. Her excuses, bad attitude, and lack of commitment to the assignments had left me no choice but to tell her this would be our last session.

I arrived at our meeting place early for some "me time" before having to confront my client. As I sat sipping on my latte, I heard laughter coming from across the street. The playground was filled with children running and skipping as though they hadn't a care in the world. I smiled at the joy and lighthearted innocence of days gone by. Why does life have to be so difficult as we grow older? Why can't we see through the lens of a child and skip through the day?

Looking a little closer, I saw three little girls playing hopscotch. I smiled as I remembered my playground years of tossing a rock and skipping from box to box. *Look at those three young girls hopping and skipping through life,* I thought to myself. Then it hit me. *Three skips and a jump and I can be there.* These young girls were showing me that the way to move through life is to skip over the things that control and cripple us, and to take a jump into the future.

Then I had an idea. I drew a hopscotch pattern on a piece of paper and picked up a rock from the ground nearby. When Emilee arrived for our coaching session, I said something to her that not only changed her life forever, it also changed the way I have approached each client from that point on.

"Emilee, are you ready to play hopscotch?"

Looking quite confused, she asked me what I was talking about. I looked straight into her eyes and said, "Are you ready to skip over your excuses and jump into your future? If not, I think we are done here."

I'm not sure if it was the illustration or the timing, but with tears forming in her eyes, she picked up the rock from the table and said to me, "Let's play."

OVERVIEW

As a Life Coach and pastor's wife, I have heard my fair share of stories from women who have felt stuck in their lives. Some have been empty nest moms looking for their identities. Some have been college graduates still looking for passion; others have gone through divorce and are ready to pick up and move on. Many are women who have been hurt, disappointed, rejected, and lied to. But they all have one thing in common: the desire for change.

We all have struggled at times with feeling inadequate, unworthy, unskilled, or lost. Our girlfriends seem to know where they are going and have a well thought-out plan for getting there. Some women seem to transition from one phase of life to another seamlessly. They appear to have all the steps planned and it's a hop, skip, and a jump into yet another perfect phase of life. Let me reassure you, this is rarely the case. Most women have great thoughts and plans for their future, but lack the tools and encouragement to get there. In this book I will lead you page by page through the steps required to become the woman God created you to be—a Woman of Influence.

A Woman of Influence has an intentional strategy for discovering her worth and identity. She recognizes that setbacks and struggles will come but she has a destiny that guides her path. She knows others are looking to her for leadership and instruction and finds great enthusiasm in her task. I believe three skips and a jump is the perfect way to discover your calling to become a Woman of Influence.

I assume you have picked up this book because you desire to either become a Woman of Influence, or you hope to define just what a Woman of Influence might look like. I am sure you are thinking to yourself, *Can it really be that easy? Three skips and a jump and voilà,*

I'm there, a Woman of Influence? Let me reassure you, the skips aren't easy and the jump is big. But yes, you can become that woman with the right attitude and correct choices. By skipping over the things that hold you back and jumping into your giftedness, you will be well on your way to becoming the woman God intended you to be.

Here's a preview of the journey to come:

SECTION A: Skip the Drama

A Woman of Influence chooses to skip over the drama of daily life. In order to do that, you must:

CHAPTER ONE: Skip the Entitlement: A Woman of Influence recognizes the areas in which she feels entitled, lets go of these things, and serves others instead.

CHAPTER TWO: Skip the Resentment: A Woman of Influence identifies the people she resents and the memories she's holding on to and learns to release the pain and control in order to let grace and forgiveness in.

CHAPTER THREE: Skip the Punishment: A Woman of Influence stops finding fault with others and herself, forgives past wrongs, and is more patient in the present and future.

SECTION B: Jump into the Future

A Woman of Influence makes up her mind to take calculated risks and does not fear her future. To do this, you must:

CHAPTER FOUR: Have a Plan: A Woman of Influence must accept the challenge to move into her divine destiny, take uncom-fortable risks to get there, and focus on discipline to stay on task. However, the reward for the challenges, risks, and discipline is a clear, well-reasoned plan.

CHAPTER FIVE: Exercise Faith: A Woman of Influence must exercise her faith and trust in God's plan and timing to see her dreams and ideas become reality.

CHAPTER SIX: Enjoy the Journey: A Woman of Influence learns to embrace each day to the fullest, living in the present rather than dwelling in the past or worrying about the future.

SECTION C: Become a Woman of Influence

A Woman of Influence understands she is fearfully and wonderfully made by God, who has a perfect plan for her life. To learn this, you must:

CHAPTER SEVEN: Recognize Your Worth: A Woman of Influence recognizes her worth and value. She has been bought with the price of God.

CHAPTER EIGHT: Embrace Your Identity: A Woman of Influence understands her physical identity, which is a product of her experiences and personalities, and her spiritual identity, which comes from her relationship with Christ.

CHAPTER NINE: Discover Your Destiny: A Woman of Influence discovers that her talents, abilities, desires, and opportunities are all woven together in the predestined plan of God: His destiny for her.

Now I'm asking you, like I asked Emilee, "Are you ready to play?" If you're ready to let go of your excuses and take a big jump into your future, you, my friend, are on your way to becoming a *Woman of Influence.*

SKIP THE DRAMA

skip (verb): to pass from one point, thing, or subject, to another, disregarding or omitting what intervenes.

A WOMAN OF INFLUENCE
chooses to skip over the daily drama of life.

"I refuse to be an actor in your drama, when I did not audition for that part."

Unknown

CHAPTER ONE

SKIP ENTITLEMENT

entitlement   (noun): the condition of having a right

to have, do, or get something; the feeling or belief that you
deserve to be given something (such as special privileges).

Do nothing out of selfish ambition or vain conceit. Rather,
in humility value others above yourselves. *Philippians 2:3 (NIV)*

The feeling of entitlement has become a part of our culture in the 21st
century. We have created a culture of "personal rights" and "expectations."
On a daily basis we witness the actions taken by those feeling entitled to a
certain behavior. Comments like "I have a right to be happy" or "I'm special
and different from everyone around me" have set the course for a society
severely lacking in consideration for one another.

I'm not sure when or how this mindset came about; maybe it's always
been at the heart of humanity. I do believe, however, we have seen an increase
in entitlement over the last several decades. I, for one, am guilty of wanting
to give my children all the blessings of a life not afforded to me. We could
say it was Generation Y's need for acceptance and approval, but then again,
it was the parenting of earlier generations that fueled the flame.

The 1980s were filled with words of affirmation and exaltation.[1] We
as parents wanted to build our children up and convince them there was
nothing they could not do or could not have. With phrases like "the sky's
the limit" and "because you're worth it," we set our children on the course
of believing they deserved only the best of everything. This attitude has
transferred outside of the home to school, sports, clubs, events, etc. Every
child gets an award for participating; every child is unique and special.

The Internet is full of stories, resources, opinions, and reasons why "I have the right to…" While researching for this chapter I came across topics like:

- I'm entitled to my opinion.
- I'm entitled to my thoughts.
- I'm entitled to wear what I want.
- I'm entitled to say what I want.
- I'm entitled to my rights.
- I'm entitled to have a gun.
- I'm entitled to have government assistance.

The list is endless, but let's look at a few areas of entitlement that plague our society today.

ENTITLED TO A COLLEGE EDUCATION

Several years ago I lived in a community next door to Morristown, New Jersey, so when the story of an eighteen-year-old young lady from that town hit the news, I was intrigued. Rachel Canning was suing her parents after allegedly being kicked out of her house for numerous bad choices. She was demanding financial support for college.[2] From what I read, the parents were flabbergasted. They reported their home is a good home with healthy rules. When their daughter began making poor decisions, they addressed her behavior, which included being suspended from school, drinking, losing her position as cheerleading captain, and being asked to leave the campus ministry.[3] The young lady moved in with her close friend and was being represented by the friend's father who is an attorney. The part that concerns me the most is that this has the potential to set a standard for similar cases— other children might decide they too can move out of their parents' homes and be entitled to financial support.

A college education is an opportunity that not everyone has, and parents are not required to support their children through college. If parents finance college, it is a gift, not a right. Eighteen-year-olds are legal adults, and most are capable of earning wages or taking out loans to fund their own education, if that is their desire for their future. When children grow up expecting that college will be paid for, they can take that opportunity for granted, whether they are aware of it or not. Paying for your own education puts a different value on it—every hour in class or grade on a midterm represents hours spent at a job or money that could be paying bills. Those who are lucky enough to be supported in part by their parents should be thankful.

Once you open yourself up to what you think you deserve, your mind starts to fill up with thoughts of entitlement. The enemy wants to fill our minds with selfishness and pride. He is seeking someone to devour.

> Be alert and of sober mind. Your enemy the devil prowls around like a roaring lion looking for someone to devour.
> *1 Peter 5:8 (NIV)*

ENTITLED IN THE WORKPLACE

Gen Y's sense of entitlement to education has carried over to employment. An article in the *The Wall Street Journal* discusses a radical attitude shift is taking place in management.[4] Many corporations are hiring consultants to train managers to become more complimentary toward their employees. There are reports of young employees becoming disillusioned and discouraged if they do not receive constant affirmation in the form of emails, rewards, prizes, and recognition for their work.

I have had the opportunity to work with some wonderful companies doing executive coaching, but it never ceases to amaze me how much "stroking employees" has to happen in today's culture. Many young workers have the attitude that if they don't like their job, they should just quit. And if one needs help quitting or getting even with an employer, just turn to Facebook. Feeling entitled to tell your boss just how you really feel? Go Social. Employees are now using Facebook to quit their jobs. A blog with a tagline of "Insightful stuff to boost your career" offers you "Ten ways to use Facebook to quit or get yourself fired, which is, after all, just a less direct way of quitting." The first five are considered the more direct methods:

- Post a message on the company's wall.
- Facebook message your boss.
- Post "I quit" on your personal wall and tag your boss.

- For subtlety, just post the company logo on your wall and say, "This is the company I used to work for."
- Mention your new job on your wall and your old company will eventually hear about it. [5]

WOW! Please tell me people aren't really doing this. When our society feels they have a right to quit a job through Facebook, we have a problem. What has happened to us? How did we get so far from doing the right thing? How did this spirit of entitlement invade our culture?

ENTITLED WITH FAMILY

In Genesis 31 we read an interesting story of a daughter's feelings toward her father. Rachel felt she did not get what she was entitled to as Laban's daughter. She had waited patiently for Jacob to become her husband and to be set free from her father's demanding hold on their lives. Then she found the time to get even. She stole his household idols and then lied about not having them when she was asked.

> Are we not regarded by him as foreigners? For he has sold us, and he has indeed devoured our money. All the wealth that God has taken away from our father belongs to us and to our children. And Rachel had stolen the household idols that were her father's. *Genesis 31:15-16, 19 (ESV)*

Jacob had met Rachel when he was in a foreign country as he fled from his brother's threat to kill him. Meeting Rachel at the local watering hole, he immediately felt swept off his feet. This was the woman for him, and he committed to marry her on the spot. What he did not know was the custom (so the father said) of marrying off the older, "not so pretty" sister first. (Sounds like a father's strategy to marry off two daughters with one son-in-law to me.)

Laban's trickery continued from one thing to another until Jacob finally reached his limit. After serving and blessing Laban's family for many years, Jacob had had enough. He made plans to steal away in the night with his two wives, livestock, and material possessions, risking his very life.

When Rachel got wind of the plan, she took it one step further, stealing her father's idols. Now I'm not sure if Rachel did this to get even with her daddy or because she truly wanted the foreign idols, but either way, it was stealing. When her father finally caught up to the caravan on the run, he asked Jacob about the idols. Jacob, having no knowledge about the stolen idols, defended his family and gave Laban permission to search the tents. One by one Daddy Laban searched the tents looking for his stolen treasures. He finally made his way to Rachel's tent. Now, this Rachel was one sneaky lady. She sat herself down on the covered idols and when asked to stand up, she replied, "I cannot, for the manner of women is with me." How clever was that? I have heard of excuses for a woman's monthly cycle, but that was genius.

What drives a person to justify a lie? Entitlement will do it every time. Rachel felt justified in her lie because she felt she deserved something. She had feelings of rejection, betrayal, anger, and pain. She must have felt very entitled to what she'd taken because if those idols had been discovered, the cost would have been her life.

Once you **open yourself** up to what you think you deserve, **your mind** starts to fill up with thoughts of entitlement.

At the time of a parent or relative's passing, have you experienced a sibling or relative complaining about not receiving something they felt entitled to? Or did you feel that you didn't get something you were expecting, whether it was money or Grandmother's favorite cherry rocking chair? The sense of entitlement that can come out when sorting through a loved one's estate can create extreme bitterness and anger. One person might feel entitled to more if they spent more time caring for the one who passed while the other sibling was elsewhere. However, that sense of entitlement only ends in damaged relationships and material goods that you can't hold on to in the end.

Do not lay up for yourselves treasures on earth, in and steal, but lay up for yourselves treasures in heaven, where neither moth nor rust destroys and where thieves do not break in and steal. For where your treasure is, there your heart will be also. *Matthew 6:19-21 (ESV)*

ENTITLED IN MARRIAGE

Being both in ministry and a Life Coach, I am continually meeting with women struggling with marital issues. Remarks like "he cheated on me" or "he is never around when I need him" have led to long discussions on commitment and forgiveness. All relationships take work; that's why they are called relationships. It is the process of relating to one another. It doesn't happen overnight, but with a commitment to stay the course, run the race, and do the work, most marriages can be restored. The problem is often people don't have the patience, persistence, or conviction to do so. As we have watched the divorce rate climb in our culture, I believe it is due to a feeling of personal entitlement. Don't like what you have? No worries; discard it and start over. And to see that you succeed through the process, let's create an environment for you to remain happy.

I thought I had heard it all when it came to ways to heal from a divorce. Then I came across a new trend on how to move on and leave your "ex" in the dust. The Internet is full of "fun and creative" ways to move on after the love is gone. Couples divorcing over their personal "right" to happiness are now hosting "divorce parties." As a foreign concept to me, I had to check it out. Google led me to site after site of great resources on how to throw a divorce party. I even found several divorce party planners waiting to assist my every need.

> ## Whatever *reality* you are trying to escape today will inevitably be knocking at your front door tomorrow.

It saddens my heart to think we have become a society so self-centered that we celebrate separation. The pain and heartache of divorce is gut-wrenching at best. Even those in the most difficult marriages would not say "celebratory" was the word to describe their divorce.

Living in Orange County, California, I have seen more than my share of divorce. My point is not the fact that people are divorcing (that's another topic); it's that we feel entitled to do whatever makes us feel good... even at the expense of another individual. It's the mindset of *I have rights, and no one can stop me from feeling and doing as I please.* We try counselors, coaches, pastors, and mediators, but all to no avail. When someone's mind is made up and they want out, the door only points in one direction: This Way Out!

The truth of the matter is the door only leads to more areas of entitlement. Whatever reality you are trying to escape today will inevitably be knocking at your front door tomorrow. If you have the mindset that you deserve only the best things from life and others, you will never be happy in this world.

ENTIT LED TO HAPPINESS

Tanya and Lindsey were high school friends. They had been together through cheerleading, mission trips, crushes, and break ups. They were two peas in a pod. After high school, they became roommates in college. Tanya dated Rick and Lindsey dated Paul. The four of them going off to college was a dream well thought out and planned for many years. The couples would be friends for life.

In their sophomore year of college, Paul was diagnosed with a brain tumor. Needless to say, the couples were devastated. Life seemed to be on pause that year for the foursome. Late in May as the springtime flowers were blooming, Paul took his last breath and made his way from this earth to heaven.

Tanya was by Lindsey's side all summer long. Through prayer, good friends, and God's healing power, Lindsey was beginning to breathe again. It was a long summer for them all. Days were long and empty with Paul now gone. They were all looking for ways to move on.

Quietly Tanya and Rick would talk about their lives without Lindsey and Paul. It seemed wrong to even think such things, let alone make plans for a future without them.

By the end of the summer Tanya and Rick were ready to get back to school and pick up life where they had left off. They were indeed in love and making plans for a future together. Tanya was packing up her room one day when Lindsey stopped by for a shoulder to cry on. "What are you doing?"

Lindsey asked Tanya as she looked around her room.

"Packing up for school, of course," she replied.

"What do you mean?" Lindsey responded in a tone that curled the tips of Tanya's heart. "We can't go back there without Paul. What are you thinking? You are my best friend, my only friend now, how could you even think of such a thing?"

Tanya knew it would be hard to leave Lindsey. They were indeed best friends, but Tanya assumed Lindsey would be coming back to college too as planned. BFF's for life!

Much to Tanya's surprise, Lindsey marched out, not only slamming the door to her house, but also the door to her heart. It was a hard thing for Lindsey to go through and now she didn't have her best friend to process with. Tanya, however, had Rick and the crisis drew them closer together.

Only those who **don't expect** their happiness to come from another human being will **truly be happy.**

As the year went on, Tanya and Rick began to make plans for their wedding after graduation. Tanya assumed Lindsey needed time to heal and learn to find a life outside of the relationship with Paul. But that was not the case. If anything, Lindsey was becoming more and more bitter against Tanya and Rick. She even began to blame them for Paul's death. She spread unkind words to all their friends that they had pulled away far before Paul's brain tumor and were not really good friends at all. She became demanding and expected her family and friends to stop everything they were doing at any time to nurse her pain and broken heart. "It's not fair. No one understands," she would cry. "My world has been crushed and you need to feel my pain." No one could smile or laugh in her presence. Life had become cold and indifferent. Time did not heal this friendship, but divided it further. Although Lindsey was invited to Tanya and Rick's graduation, she declined.

One day Tanya stopped by Lindsey's house to share some exciting news. "Lindsey, you have been my best friend since second grade. We have shared our lives together from childhood. We have gone through hard times and happy times. I can't imagine this moment without you in my life. Lindsey, Rick has asked me to marry him, and I want you to be my maid of honor."

The expression on Lindsey's face should have been enough, but Tanya had hoped that would not be the case. "Maid-of-honor, *maid-of-honor*? Are you kidding me? What kind of person are you? I lose the man of my dreams and my hope for a future, while you go on and act as though he never existed. Aren't I entitled to happiness? Aren't I entitled to a husband, college, and a life ever after? What about my life? Aren't I entitled too?"

Entitlement will kill your hopes and dreams. It is the belief you deserve what someone else has. Although my heart breaks for situations like Lindsey and Paul, life is unfair at times, and only those who don't expect their happiness to come from another human being will truly be happy.

To my knowledge Tanya and Lindsey have not reconciled their friendship. This story happens more often than you may think. Maybe it's part of your story, too.

HOW TO SKIP **ENTITLEMENT**

Entitlement is a curse on our culture today. It can stem from the child who doesn't feel they were given enough opportunities, to the divorced partner that didn't get their fair share. Entitlement says you deserve something other than that what you have been given.

Women of Influence choose to skip over entitlement. *But how do I do that?* you may be asking yourself. Here are five ways to deal with entitlement: Read each one slowly and ask yourself if you are ready to move past feelings of entitlement.

1. Admit You Have Feelings of Entitlement

Be honest with yourself and don't sugarcoat the issue. That's how we have gotten to the point we are at today. I must admit I am guilty of the feeling of entitlement. I was driving home from work one afternoon when quite abruptly, the traffic came to a stop. As I waited patiently for the traffic to pick up, a car came along side of me to merge into my lane. *I don't think so, buddy...*was my first thought. Actually, it was my only thought. *I was here first. I waited patiently in line. You can just get behind me and wait your turn.* There, I said it. I admit I have feelings of entitlement. I will, however, say that when I got home I felt horrible. *What is wrong with me?* I questioned. *How did I get so selfish as to not let someone go in front of me?* This is an area I know I have to release to God and allow a spirit of consideration to take over. I believe much of the road rage we see today is evidence of the spirit of entitlement. Not until you admit you have times of entitlement, will you ever truly be gracious. Mark Twain put it best when he said, "Don't go around saying the world owes you a living. The world owes you nothing. It was here first."

2. Have a Servant's Attitude

This is a hard concept for many people to embrace. Most of us have a hard enough time doing our own job, let alone helping others with theirs. Such was the case with our staff before they understood a servant's attitude. It is so easy to walk by a need when it is not on your job description. Often we justify that is not our responsibility, so we blindly walk by without even noticing the need.

My husband shared a story with our staff one day about a small tree limb that had fallen in front of the church door. As he watched from inside he observed person after person stepping right over the limb and walking into the church. So he thought he would do a little test. He attached a five-dollar bill to the tree limb to see if anyone would stop and move the obstruction from the door. The next person to walk up to the door saw the five-dollar bill wrapped around the limb, so they took the money stepped over the limb and walked through the door. Excited to have found a five-dollar bill, the person bragged about his newfound treasure, only to discover it represented his lack of a servant's attitude. I think we all have had times of stepping over jobs to be done. Part of it is laziness and part entitlement, but the truth is, we need a servant's attitude. If there is a job to be done, just do it. Don't wait to be asked; take the initiative and develop the heart of a servant. Jesus said it best in Matthew 20:26, "Whoever wants to become great among you must be your servant" (NIV).

3. Encourage Others to Help

We have become a lazy society. People have an attitude of *how can I get out?* instead of *how can I help out?* Everyone can do more. I love the way Bob Proctor put it, "It doesn't matter where you are; you are nowhere compared to where you can go." I love being a Life Coach; the joy I receive as I equip and encourage women to seize the opportunities God has given them is thrilling. I truly believe deep down people want to be a blessing and make a difference; they just need encouragement and instruction.

> It doesn't matter **where you are;**
> you are nowhere compared to
> **where you can go.**

My good friend Caitlin Crosby is a great example of encouraging others. She started a company called The Giving Keys[6] that has transformed lives and encouraged countless individuals. It started in New York with her hotel room key. Caitlin is an actress and singer/songwriter and had the idea to start engraving old used keys with inspirational words. She realized that in a way we are all like these keys—unique, flawed, scarred, and at risk of being discarded—and she wanted these keys to have their purpose renewed over and over again. Their message is yours for a time, but once they've served their purpose with you, you are to pay it forward to inspire another. Looking for someone to help her produce the endless demand for orders, she saw a homeless couple sitting on the side of the road in Hollywood, California. Realizing this was just what she was looking for, she asked them to join her in making keys that would make a difference by encouraging others.

Today the couple is off the street; they have their own apartment and are happily employed. There is no telling what can happen when you open your eyes to see how you can encourage others. Maybe you can start by giving a key away to someone who needs some encouragement.

There are wonderful organizations and movements making a difference in our world today. Our task is to join their efforts and enlist others to join as well. There is a great quote I use often: "Make your life a mission—not an intermission" (Author Unknown).

Make your life a **mission—**
not an **intermission.**

As we begin to change our attitude about what we should and should not do, others will see our example and follow suit. If they don't, don't give up; just continue to encourage them along the way.

4. Be Countercultural

Unfortunately our society has become indifferent and often ignorant to the needs of others. Something simple like holding the door for another person, or allowing someone with a crying child to go ahead of you in the supermarket has become a thing of the past. Things that were once considered polite have now become rights. But I believe people are looking for leaders—people who are willing to forge ahead and take a stand and to demonstrate kindness and respect for others. Ralph Waldo Emerson said, "The world makes way for the man who knows where he is going." Don't blend into culture; stand out with conviction. Trendsetters are needed to pave the way toward kindness and away from self-centeredness. I have two very good friends that have started non-profit organizations to help young girls caught in the trap of human trafficking. I have a very precious friend who has created an organization to feed the homeless in LA. Our church works with The Boys and Girls Club of Anaheim to provide Christmas gifts for underprivileged kids. There is always a way to impact culture in a positive way if you are willing to work. Albert Einstein said, "Your imagination is your preview of life's coming attractions." Are you willing to imagine a change the culture of entitlement with your efforts?If so you can be countercultural.

5. Adopt A Less-is-More Attitude

When I was thirteen I went on my first mission trip to Haiti. It took me months to prepare for the adventure. I mean packing, that is. I had to think about my toiletries, of course, and then what I would wear, what food I would bring, and it goes without mention, I was concerned about what I would do with my hair. My mother and I had so much fun shopping for the perfect items for my trip. Color coordinated tops and shorts, bows and headbands, shoes and socks. I even packed a small bag with sweets and snacks in case I didn't like the food in Haiti.

As I left my home that morning I had no idea that I would not return the same person. Day after day we would travel into villages to meet the children and play games. I was heartbroken by the poverty and lack of fresh water in the villages, but also amazed to witness the joy and laughter in the hearts of the children. The kids would run towards us as though we were their best friends. They would jump and laugh out loud at the slightest little thing. There was a joy in their hearts and a smile on their faces that was foreign to us. *How can they be so happy,* I thought. *Look at their shacks, their clothes, their lack of food and water, why are they so happy?* These kids had no idea the amount of effort and time my mother and I spent getting ready for my trip. They only knew I was there—not what I was wearing or what I had spent to get there—just that I was there to play with them.

The more simplicity I see, the more of it I want. The children of Haiti touched my heart and will forever remind me that happiness does not come from materialism, but from the innermost part of my heart. I left all my new clothes, shoes, socks, and snacks with my new Haitian friends. A small group of American teens went home suitcase-less and changed forever. Going to Haiti set my high school years in motion for a heart for ministry. It impressed upon my heart the truth that less is more and more is too much. People with far less than I seem to have much more contentment.

Less is **more**
and **more** is too much.

COACHING EXERCISE

1. List four areas in which you have recognized entitlement in your personal life. *For example: An employee that doesn't respond quickly enough, a driver who cuts in front of you, someone who gets a handout for something you had to pay for, or when someone does not take care of something that belongs to you.*

    _____

    _____

    _____

    _____

    _____

    _____

    _____

    _____

2. Practice the art of allowing someone to go in front of you this week:
    - In the supermarket checkout
    - On the freeway exit ramp
    - In line at the restaurant
    - While holding the door for another

    _____

    _____

    _____

    _____

    _____

    _____

    _____

COACHING EXERCISE

3. Clean out your closet, kitchen, and garage and give away things that are not being used or needed. Write out a to-do list:

_____

_____

_____

_____

_____

_____

4. Volunteer at an organization that could use your help and assistance. Jot down a place to visit:

_____

_____

_____

_____

_____

5. Begin to mentor your children, friends, or loved ones to replace their attitude of entitlement with an attitude of generosity. Brainstorm some ideas:

_____

_____

_____

_____

_____

FOOTNOTES

[1] Check out more about this idea at: Aspen Education Group. (n.d.). Narcissistic and entitled to everything! Does Gen Y have too much self-esteem? Retrieved from http://aspeneducation.crchealth.com/articles/article-entitlement/ and Urban, Tim. (2013, September 15). Why Generation Y yuppies are unhappy. *Huffington Post: Wait But Why.* Retrieved from http://www.huffingtonpost.com/wait-but-why/generation-y-unhappy_b_3930620.html

[2] Klein, R. (2014, March 4). Rachel Canning, 18, is suing her parents for college tuition. *Huffington Post: College.* Retrieved from http://www.huffingtonpost.com/2014/03/04/rachel-canning-lawsuit_n_4896715.html

[3] Chappell, B. (2014, March 4). Teen sues parents, claiming they owe her money for college. *The Two-Way: Breaking News from NPR.* Retrieved from http://www.npr.org/blogs/thetwo-way/2014/03/04/285887838/teen-sues-parents-claiming-they-owe-her-money-for-college

[4] Zaslow, J. (2007, April 20). The most-praised generation goes to work. *The Wall Street Journal.* Retrieved from http://online.wsj.com/articles/SB117702894815776259

[5] Lewis, S. (n.d.). 10 ways to use Facebook to quit your job. *Onlymarketingcareers.* Retrieved from http://blog.onlymarketingjobs.com/10-ways-to-use-facebook-to-quit-your-job/

[6] Check out the website at http://www.thegivingkeys.com/

CHAPTER TWO

SKIP RESENTMENT

resentment (noun): a feeling of anger or displeasure about someone or something unfair.

Let all bitterness and wrath and anger and clamor and slander be put away from you, along with all malice. *Ephesians 4:31 (ESV)*

One obstacle that will keep you from becoming a Woman of Influence is resentment. The feeling of resentment translates into anger and displeasure and will cripple and control you to the point of destruction. Resentment only has one outcome for you: Death. The death of your happiness, peace, hope, and future.

Resentment doesn't happen overnight; it is the process of reliving hurtful words, actions, and behaviors over and over in your mind. Resentment grows like a vine: Once the seed is planted in your heart, it takes root and that person or event begins to control your thoughts, rule your emotions, rob you of peace, and disrupt your dreams. As the vine grows, resentment becomes your constant daily companion. It lives in your home, rides in your car, and goes on holiday with you. It sleeps with you and rises with you. Yippee! Meet your new best friend.

Maybe you struggle with resentment because you are easily offended. Maybe you take a lot of things personally and tend to wear your heart on your sleeve. Maybe someone close to you disappointed or hurt you in a way you didn't think was possible. Maybe you think God abandoned you—that when you needed Him most, He was nowhere to be found. And every day you live with resentment entwined around your soul. If you have resentment toward another person or toward God, ask yourself, *Why? Is this really worth the emotional energy it is taking on my life?*

Let's look at a few ways people experience the disease of resentment and consider healthy ways to process the hurt and anger to come out on the other side free and full of contentment.

RESENTING FRIENDS

Imagine you're out to dinner with a group of friends when someone brings up how much fun they all had at the spa last weekend. You chime in that you knew nothing about it. One friend responds, "Oh, we knew you didn't like to spend money on frivolous things, so we thought you wouldn't like to come."

First you are hurt that you were not invited, then your hurt turns to anger, and finally into resentment. You begin thinking, *Who do they think they are? I bet they really didn't want me to come in the first place.*

You go home and tell your husband what they did. He laughs and says, "Well, they are probably right. You know you don't like to spend money on things like that."

"But they should have at least asked me," you reason. "Friends include each other in everything. It should have been my choice to decide."

Now a seed of resentment has been planted in your heart, and each time you are with your friends, you recall the hurt of not being included. You replay the event over and over in your mind. After weeks of rehearsing the memory of exclusion, the seed has now been adequately fertilized, and the seedling is now a vine growing in your soul. Your friendship with the girls has changed, and you justify your disinterest of doing anything with them by saying they are shallow and selfish.

By letting this resentment take root, you are allowing bitterness and anger to rule you, which Ephesians 4:31 warns us to stay away from. The verse calls us instead to "Be kind to one another, tenderhearted, forgiving one another, as God in Christ forgave you" (ESV). Forgive your friends when you feel slighted, and if this happens again, consider saying something like, "Oh that sounds like fun… I might have just surprised you all and gone with you. Please include me next time." This addresses the issue of feeling excluded and sets a precedent to be invited even if you choose not to go.

RESENTING FAMILY

According to *Psychology Today*, "The inability to overcome resentment probably constitutes the single most devastating impediment to repairing a disintegrating intimate connection, family rift, or severed friendship."[7] I've seen the devastating outcome of resentment on many occasions in my coaching career, and one dynamic is often between parents and their children.

Susie scheduled an appointment with me to talk about a situation she found herself in with her daughter Jessica. Susie was a single mom who had to work two jobs to provide for Jessica. Susie had started a college fund when her daughter was three and continued adding from every paycheck since. By the time Jessica was a teenager, Susie had accumulated quite a large sum for her.

Susie shared with me how year after year she would tell her daughter how proud she was that one day Jessica would be able to go to college and make something of herself. She would play the dream game with her daughter, and they would pretend all the things Jessica could one day become.

Susie had high hopes for Jessica and had begun to unintentionally live her personal dreams though her daughter's life. You see, Susie never went to college. She got pregnant by her high school boyfriend, and after he threatened to leave her if she didn't get an abortion, she found herself alone with a little pink bundle in her arms.

"Education is important," Susie's parents always told her. "Stay in school, get good grades, and maybe one day you will become something." If she heard it once, she heard it a thousand times. Over and over in her mind she would replay the message from her parents. This mindset had now become the subconscious goal for her daughter.

As I listened to Susie share her heart with me, I could feel her pain. But much of her pain was self-imposed.

Susie had a picture of what life would look like for Jessica after she graduated from high school and was excited about looking for the perfect college with her daughter. Once again picking up on the hopes and dreams of her personal life, she began to impose her dreams onto Jessica. Now re-member, Susie had worked two jobs for a very long time to save for Jessica's future. She even put Jessica's name on the bank account when she turned eighteen to show her confidence in her daughter.

So it was quite a surprise when the day after Jessica graduated from high school, she withdrew all the money in the bank account and bought a condo with her boyfriend. You see, Jessica never had any intention of going to college. She was an artist who had dreams of starting her own design company with her boyfriend. Somehow while playing the dream game with Jessica, Susie never heard her daughter say she loved to design and had plans of becoming a world-renowned designer.

> ## If we can **identify** our resentment and **uncover** its source, we can uproot it and finally experience **healing & peace.**

To say that Susie resented her daughter would be an understatement. Remember, we defined resentment as a feeling of anger or displeasure about someone or something unfair. Now take that thought and multiply it by one thousand percent. Susie was so angry that she no longer wanted a relationship with her own daughter.

Resentment can kill relationships, dreams, and even your very soul. Susie sat crying as she asked me if I thought she could ever get over this.

"Over what?" I asked. "Your daughter's choice to use the money in a different manner than you had hoped for? Over the fact that Jessica did not go to college? Over the decision to move in with her boyfriend? Over the truth that Jessica is not you, and she, like you, disappointed her parents?"

It may sound direct for me to ask such tough questions, but the truth of the matter is, resentment is a feeling we nurse when we don't get things our way. As I began to work with Susie, she was able to see her own agenda in the life of her daughter. She began to process and work on her own needs of acceptance. She built a healthy bridge back into her parents' lives, and began to embrace the gifts and talents of her daughter. She learned to listen and not just talk as Jessica shared her dreams for design. She let her heart heal and found joy in hearing her daughter talk about what made her happy.

Sometimes people just need to be heard. Jessica and her mom began to reconnect and respect one another. Through coaching, Susie began to work on herself and develop healthy skills in communication. She began dating again and met a great guy who made her feel valuable. Jessica and her boyfriend broke up and she sold her condo for more money than it cost her originally, and used it to go to an art institute.

Susie was able to acknowledge her resentment, examine where it was coming from, address the past hurt in her own life, then repair her relationship with her daughter. If we can identify our resentment and uncover its source, we can uproot it and finally experience healing and peace. But sometimes, letting go isn't that simple.

RESENTING GOD

The Bible gives us examples of women who resented God. Consider Genesis 16, when we read of Sarai's struggle with being barren. Sarai was Abram's wife and she was loved deeply by him. She had his heart, attention, and affection, but she did not have any of his children. Being barren was considered a curse, and Sarai may have struggled already with resentment before the angel of the Lord came to Abram in his old age. The angel told him that they would have a son and have more descendants than stars in the skies, but Sarai did not believe it could be so. There is nothing more frustrating than when God tells you to believe and trust Him for something— to just have patience and a little faith—yet your circumstances say something else. Sarai resented her barrenness and probably resented God for seeming to taunt her with this prophecy.

Sarai had a handmaiden, Hagar, and Sarai told Abram to father a child with Hagar so that the prophecy could come true. If God was not going to act on her behalf, then she would have to take matters into her own hands.

Now Sarai, Abram's wife, had borne him no children. But she had an Egyptian slave named Hagar; so she said to Abram, "The Lord has kept me from having children. Go, sleep with my slave; perhaps I can build a family through her." *Genesis 16:1-2 (NIV)*

What was Sarai thinking? She desired a family so badly and was so worried about being barren that she thought she was the one who would have to make the prophecy come true. She didn't realize that God didn't need any help and that He had His own plan. God was revealing His power and His covenant by giving her and Abram a child. Instead of trusting that God was powerful, she stuck her hands into things and ended up making Israel's history a lot more complicated. Hagar's son, Ishmael, became the father of a separate nation that would always "live in hostility toward his brothers" *(Genesis 16:12, NIV)*. Sarai should have trusted God, even in her barrenness, rather than letting her resentment about her situation guide her.

I've also seen women who feel like they can't trust God, like His promises won't come true for them. I've seen women come to resent God for the pain they've had to experience in their lives, pain that was beyond their control.

Sometimes we experience situations in our lives that make no sense to us. Things happen to us that just seem incongruous with God's love. Maybe you grew up in a home where you were verbally abused—where you were told you were stupid, ugly, fat, or clumsy, never as good as your siblings, or just plain never good enough. Maybe you've been in a relationship with someone who hit you, pushed you around, or truly frightened you. Maybe someone took advantage of you. Maybe someone close to you died, was killed, or took their own life. So many things can happen that can make us feel like God doesn't know us or care about us, and we can resent Him and everyone around us for it.

Olivia was a freshman in college when I met her. She had a lot of reasons to resent God and the things that had happened in her life. Her first weekend of college, she flew home for the sentencing. It was a plea bargain, and Olivia didn't have to testify, but she could take the stand. She read a letter to the judge. She told the judge she wanted the defendant to serve ten years for the ten years he was married to her sister, Marie, three years for the three years he'd taken from her, and another seven or so in case he ever thought of even looking at another underage girl again.

Then Olivia had to sit down and listen as women from his work took the stand and said they would trust him with their teenage daughters. She had to listen to him take the stand and say it was all a mistake. She watched him receive his sentence, thirty months, and be cuffed and led out of the room, but then saw her father hug him in the hallway.

Larry first became part of Olivia's family when Olivia was five and Larry was sixteen. Larry dated Olivia's older sister, Marie, through high school and into college. Larry was always at the house as Olivia grew up, and he would play with her when no one else would. He went on family vacations, and his parents were friends with Olivia and Marie's parents. Eventually, Larry and Marie got married. Right before Olivia turned thirteen, Larry started paying a lot more attention to Olivia. And initially Olivia loved the attention because she was barely a teenager, awkward, and insecure. But Larry's attention became more keen, more intense, more intimate. And that attention developed into three and a half years of dark, suffocating sexual abuse.

During those years, Olivia would pray to God to make it end. She was a Christian, and she felt that it was her fault that the relationship was happening. She thought if she told anyone, the families would fall apart, her world would fall apart, and everyone would hate her. So she kept it together, and the summer before her junior year of high school, she finally cut off contact with Larry.

She told her family she just didn't want to see him anymore. They were all relieved because they thought the relationship was awkward, at best. No one asked too many questions at first. But then finally someone did ask. And she couldn't deny it. She tried. But as it came out, Olivia's parents asked her how she could have let it happen. Her parents would not press charges against Larry; it eventually made it to the police because someone heard who was a state-mandated reporter. Marie left him, but would not speak to Olivia.

The case took almost two years to prosecute, and instead of feeling a sense of justice, Olivia just felt guilty. She knew she should be glad it went to court and he went to jail, but she didn't feel like her family was on her side, even though they tried to be. She knew she should feel like justice had been served, but she didn't. She was worried she had ruined her family, and she felt they blamed her for what had happened. They were Christians, and they seemed to expect her as a Christian to have "ended it" before it even started.

Olivia and I spent a lot of time working on resentment. She resented

Larry, she resented her body, she resented her parents, her siblings, the court system, and she resented God and His plan for her life.... It took a lot of digging to get to the root of the problems and the emotions involved, and even more time for healing to begin.

No matter what kind of resentment
you are harboring, no matter how deeply
it is rooted in your heart, you can choose
to **skip over resentment** and move
forward in your journey to becoming
a Woman of Influence.

I can tell you that Olivia is now a happy, healthy young woman, but it was not an easy journey. The resentment that is bound up in the pain of abuse is difficult to overcome. But she did, and you can do it, too.

No matter what kind of resentment you are harboring, no matter how deeply it is rooted in your heart, you can choose to skip over resentment and move forward in your journey to becoming a Woman of Influence. The first and most important step is to admit that you are harboring resentment. Then you must take action to uncover the seed that started it, seek understanding, release the hurt, let go of any desires for revenge, forgive the one who hurt you, and practice grace as you begin a life free of resentment. Let's look at these steps a little more closely.

SEVEN STEPS TO LETTING GO OF RESENTMENT

1. Admit resentment is a poison to your soul.
The effects of resentment to your body are alarming: lack of sleep, high blood pressure, hyperventilation, mood swings, eating disorders, and the list goes on. When we allow resentment to reside in our lives, we are hurting ourselves. Admit you are allowing another person to live in your body without your permission.

2. Uncover the seed of resentment.

What is at the root of your resentment? What event set it all off? We all have experienced times of misunderstanding or even rudeness—the insensitive comment of a close friend or a forgotten special occasion. Some of us have experienced abuse in different forms. Regardless of the source, you must uncover that seed to understand where your hurt and pain are coming from. If you don't understand how resentment begins, it's like pulling dandelions from your yard but only plucking the flowers.

Resentment typically starts with a hurtful feeling that turns into anger. It is at that point you must recognize the emotion and deal with it. Stop the thought before it grows any deeper. The key to success is to stop the emotion between hurt and anger, and to recognize the seed before it grows into fully rooted resentment.

Learn to discern the difference between anger and resentment, as well.

EVENT > HURT > ANGER > RESENTMENT

Look after each other so that none of you fails to receive the grace of God. Watch out that no poisonous root of bitterness grows up to trouble you, corrupting many. *Hebrews 12:15 (NLT)*

3. Try to understand the other person's side.

Put yourself in the shoes of the one who hurt you. Does it look different from their side? In the example of the friends who went to the spa, they made a decision based on what they thought another friend would want. The truth was they did not want to put her in an embarrassing position to have to say she did not want to go. Together they reasoned that was the best option. Before we react and respond to our emotional feeling, we need to think it through.

Whoever is slow to anger has great understanding, but he who has a hasty temper exalts folly. *Proverbs 14:29 (ESV)*

4. Release the hurt you are feeling into the hands of God.

Let's be honest: Even though a good friend can sympathize with your experience, they cannot do anything to heal it. God has the power and remedy to heal. Pain hurts, and God alone understands your deepest emotion. There is something very powerful about releasing your innermost conflicts to God. Not only are you admitting that He is capable of carrying them, but you are receiving the healing power that He alone can give.

Humble yourselves, therefore, under God's mighty hand, that he may lift you up in due time. Cast all your anxiety on him because he cares for you. *I Peter 5:6-7 (NIV)*

5. Let go of your need for revenge.

When we are hurt and angry, often one of our desires is to punish the person who hurt us. Sometimes this just means insulting a person who insulted us or cutting off the car who cut us off, but sometimes we want vengeance for the crimes that have hurt much deeper, like in Olivia's case. However, God is ultimately the one who judges each person for their actions and who will carry out justice, not us. In Romans 12:19, Paul writes, "Do not take revenge, my dear friends, but leave room for God's wrath, for it is written: "It is mine to avenge; I will repay," says the Lord" (NIV). In the next chapter, we will look at punishment as one of the obstacles that prevents us from becoming Women of Influence. Until then, remember:

See that no one repays anyone evil for evil, but always seek to do good to one another and to everyone. *I Thessalonians 5:15 (ESV)*

6. Forgive the person that offended you.

Forgiveness is the balm of life. In Colossians 3:13 we read: "Bear with each other and forgive one another if any of you has a grievance against someone. Forgive as the Lord forgave you" (NIV). I don't know about you, but I love to be forgiven. The feeling of release and freedom when I know someone has granted me forgiveness is a balm to my soul. "Bear with each other" means help each other, carry the weight, and feel the pain of the process. Then we must forgive one another. I think God understands the human heart better than all of us. He knew that it would take forgiveness on the part of both parties to truly experience freedom. The human heart only has so much capacity. Don't fill it up with resentment toward another human being. Let go of the hurt, pain, and memories that you have experienced and make room for the goodness of God in your heart.

7. Practice grace.

The truth is, people hurt people. Even you have hurt others, and others have had to forgive you. "All have sinned and fall short of the glory of God" (Romans 3:23, NIV), but God has given grace to all who believe in Him, and He expects you to share His grace with those around you. To be free of resentment, we must learn to offer grace to those who don't deserve it: Even when we're hurt, even when we feel angry, and especially when we're hurt and feel angry. A Woman of Influence practices grace to begin a life free from resentment.

Let your speech always be gracious, seasoned with salt, so that you may know how you ought to answer each person. *Colossians 4:6 (ESV)*

These steps to letting go of resentment will not be easy, and some steps will be much harder than others. However, God has called you to forgive others as He forgave you, and He will strengthen you as you make the choice to skip over resentment and move forward in your journey to becoming a Woman of Influence.

This next coaching exercise may be very difficult and takes some time. It requires honesty as you examine your memories and your emotions. However, I believe you will find it rewarding—you are traveling the path to a life free from the things that have been holding you back. Let go of resentment and experience the freedom of God's forgiveness and grace.

COACHING EXERCISE

1. Get some paper out and make a list of three to five people who have caused you hurt or pain.

2. Now write one paragraph telling each of them how you feel.

3. Ask yourself if you are willing to forgive them and be set free.

4. If you answered yes, then write them a letter telling them you forgive them.

5. Now destroy the letters. The exercise is for you to experience freedom. Your actions of forgiveness will speak louder than any words you could ever write.

FOOTNOTES

[7] Sichel, M. (2011, March 3). Living with resentment is like taking poison and hoping the other guy will get sick. *Psychology Today*. Retrieved from http://www.psychologytoday.com/blog/the-therapist-is-in/201103/living-resentment-is-taking-poison-and-hoping-the-other-guy-will-get

CHAPTER THREE

SKIP PUNISHMENT

punishment (noun): suffering, pain, or loss that serves as retribution; severe, rough, or disastrous treatment.

For as high as the heavens are above the earth, so great is His steadfast love toward those who fear Him; as the east is from the west, so far does He remove our transgressions from us.
Psalm 103:11-12 (ESV)

In working with people over the last thirty years I have witnessed many women punishing those around them, as well as punishing themselves. The punishment takes different forms and we act out different roles, but we are just using different means to achieve the same end—to make someone pay who hurt us or who we think needs correction.

Some of us use punishment to repay the deep resentment we carry, hurting those who have hurt us by whatever means available. Others feel it is our duty as Christians or good citizens to point out others' sins and shortcomings and to pass out punishment so that the offenders will learn a valuable lesson. Some of us punish those who are closest to us by withholding pleasure—love, affection, sex, attention, time—to repay hurt feelings or to redirect blame from ourselves to someone else. Sometimes we punish ourselves because we feel guilty, and we use negative self-talk or abuse our bodies. However, punishment—whether towards another person or self-inflicted—is never the way to move forward. Punishment keeps us focused on the past, but a Woman of Influence chooses to skip punishment and focus on the healthier, happier life she can have through God's forgiveness and grace.

It's been said, "The first to apologize is the bravest, the first to forgive is the strongest, and the first to forget is the happiest.

PUNISHING OURSELVES

One way we use punishment is to direct it inward, toward ourselves. When we struggle with forgiving ourselves for something that has happened, or when we don't know how to process our emotions, we may take that turmoil and focus it inward. Some people punish themselves with negative self-talk, tearing themselves down with every thought. Others punish themselves by withholding food, abusing alcohol or drugs, inflicting bodily self-harm, engaging in harmful relationships—the list could go on about all the ways we find to punish ourselves. While you can hide the ways you're abusing yourself for a while, eventually the results will show, as Cammy found out.

Cammy's love for pageants began when she was five years old. Well, maybe it was her mother's love at first. Cammy shared with me that she loved the thrill of competition. Beauty, skill, ability, and poise were on her side, along with a personality that was irresistible. What was not to love about Cammy? At first the pageants were fun and a great resource for self-esteem. Cammy's mom knew she was a natural and would always tell others, "Who knows, maybe this could even open up doors of opportunity for her in the future."

As Cammy met with personal coaches, advisers, consultants, and fashion experts growing up, she began to realize she was on the fast track to success. What Cammy did not expect was the pressure to look like someone she was not.

Exercise, diet, fashion, and performance seemed to be the bywords of the household. Size two seemed reasonable to Cammy, but not to her training coach. "Come on, Cammy, really you must lose a little more weight for the camera; you're beautiful, but your abs need to be more pronounced for the swimsuit competition."

Oooohh! *Competition*, the one word that would always make Cammy work a little harder, get up a little earlier, eat a little less, and perform a little better. Cammy was addicted to competition, the thrill of success, the feeling that you are the best and no one can compare to you. By eighteen, Cammy had seen her share of the limelight. She had won crowns and received roses. She had experienced the thrill of winning and the rewards of working hard. Cammy was on top of the world.

By twenty-two the competitions were beginning to take a toll on Cammy's body. She had misused and undernourished herself to the point of exhaustion. Believing that if she just worked a little harder she could compete again in the summer pageant led Cammy on the most rigorous program thus far. Even Cammy's mom was getting worried for her daughter.

Cammy was becoming irrational and angry. Her workouts and diet program were so aggressive that her fitness coaches threatened to get her help if she did not gain some weight. Cammy refused to listen and continued to train harder and eat less.

Some people **punish themselves** with negative self-talk, tearing themselves down with every thought.

One day a good friend of mine asked me if I would meet with Cammy for personal coaching. I agreed to meet with her if she was willing to do the assignments I gave her each week. Surprisingly the answer from Cammy that came back was "NO!"; she was insulted someone would even suggest she needed help, especially from a Life Coach. Her life was perfect. She was on a path that would lead to her hopes and dreams, and if her "friend" could not see that, then she was no friend at all. Funny how those looking at us can often see us better than we can see ourselves, or at least better than we may want to see ourselves.

The summer was quickly fading and the pageant was approaching. Cammy was exhausted but convinced she never looked better. Her friends and family had taken a back seat in her life, due to both her insane personal schedule and her constant complaints that no one really ever supported her dreams.

The day finally came for the pageant and Cammy was glowing. Most people believed it was her spray tan. But Cammy rolled her eyes and replied, "Just have your cameras ready when I am crowned."

Out of the many pageants Cammy had entered, there was never a time she did not receive a crown, or at least make it to the top five. She was a natural beauty and her poise took over from there.

Only the camera could really capture the expression of rejection, pain, and embarrassment on Cammy's face when her name was not called with the first list of girls. Gracefully walking off stage, Cammy faced the realization that she had a problem and needed some real help.

Cammy's life spiraled out of control. Depression set in, and she would not get out of bed for days. She rehearsed over and over in her mind what she did wrong. *Was I too fat? Was I too thin? Was it my question? Was it my answer? Why have I spent my life in this crazy industry?* Cammy was already anorexic, but now she was becoming bulimic. She had ostracized herself from any friends and said she did not deserve to have friends after the way she had acted.

Cammy began losing chunks of hair due to her diet and stress, which led to more unhealthy behavior. Feeling alone and ugly, Cammy resorted to cutting herself as a way of self-punishment for her behavior. Cammy's world was caving in on her, and this once beautifully poised princess was now contemplating ending her very life.

Psychology Today defines self-harm as the deliberate infliction of damage to your own body, and it includes cutting, burning, and other forms of injury.[8] While cutting can look like attempted suicide, it's not; most people who mutilate themselves do it as a way to regulate mood. People who hurt themselves in this way may be motivated by a need to distract themselves from inner turmoil, or to quickly release anxiety that builds due to an inability to express intense emotions.

When I first met Cammy, I saw a girl full of self-hatred that had turned into self-punishment. She felt like a failure and believed she did not deserve happiness or success. She felt good when she blamed herself because often this was the only feeling she had. She had brought this upon herself and now she was forced to live with it. Punishment was the tool she used on herself for losing the pageant and treating her friends so badly. It all made sense in her head, and that was where she was currently living.

It was not an easy road for Cammy, but within several weeks she started to see some improvement. The biggest battle for Cammy was in her mind; it was the way she saw herself. She had not understood that she was created in the image of an all-loving God who knows her name. She heard that she was priceless and adored because of who she is, not what she does. Cammy began to read the love book of God (the Bible) and meditate on His Holy Scriptures. She gave her life to the One who gives life, and she found love everlasting. Not only did Cammy understand her worth and value from God, but also she discovered her gifts and talents. Through personal assignments and assessments, Cammy did the work necessary to not only heal from her past, but also to thrive in her future.

PUNISHING OTHERS FOR OUR PAIN

Another way we use punishment is when we take the pain we're experiencing and direct it toward someone else. The subconscious mind says, *It's not my fault. Someone or something has caused this pain in my life.* Because we don't want to deal with that pain, we try to transfer it to another place. We struggle with taking responsibility for our feelings, just like Joyce did.

Joyce was like a lot of young women growing up in a church environment— she had a desire for a Christian husband. She longed for someone with whom she could be equally yoked, who had a good work ethic, was from a good family, and shared an interest in the outdoors and having fun together.

When Joyce met Ben, she thought her prayers were answered. Good guy, good home, cute, fun, good job, and most importantly, he was a Christian.

Joyce and Ben fell in love, and after setting a wedding date, they began their marital counseling. Life quickly fell in place after the honeymoon, and seven short months after they were married, Joyce was pregnant. Excitement filled the air as Ben and Joyce began to prepare their home for the new arrival. Mike was born first at 9 lbs. 7 oz., and fifteen months later, Leslie came into the world at 9 lbs. 2 oz.

Joyce was on top of the moon. Her dream for a good man and children had come faster than she thought, but she was not complaining. Fortunately, Ben had a great job and Joyce had the privilege of staying home with the kids.

She was a great mom. Stories, dress up, parks, and adventures were their everyday routine. Joyce enjoyed her kids so much she decided to homeschool them through elementary school and then she would determine whether to continue through junior high and, who knows, maybe even high school.

Life was going great for Joyce and her family. The only area that was a struggle for Joyce was her weight. Having two kids so close together, and large babies at that, gave Joyce an excuse for gaining weight. The other problem was that Joyce loved to cook for her family. At first it was an adventure playing house with a husband and two kids. But before long, Joyce began to feel the pain of her weight. Ben would make comments about "the good old days when we could both fit in the recliner together" or, "Remember when you wore those cute little summer dresses?"

Another way we use **punishment** is when we take the pain we're experiencing and **direct** it toward someone else.

Joyce began to resent her husband. Didn't he understand how hard it was to get your body back after having a baby? In Joyce's eyes, children were the highest gift from God, and Ben should just be happy she was such a great wife. She would drop hints here and there about how lucky Ben was to have a wife willing to stay home and raise his children. The fact that when he came home each night he had dinner on the table and well-disciplined children to greet him should count for something. She kept a clean and happy home— what more could he want?

Little by little Joyce's resentment turned to anger. She would lash out with her words and gestures to let Ben know she was not happy with him. In her desire to punish Ben for his comments, Joyce was sabotaging herself. You see, Joyce also had a stubborn streak. She had reasoned that if Ben didn't love her for who God had made her to be, then his love was not real.

Now, as Joyce's Life Coach I had told Joyce the truth that if she did not truly value and respect herself, no one else would. Joyce had come to me for personal identity coaching in hopes to develop a healthy self-view. The problem was Joyce was using the self-identity tools as a way to justify her anger toward her spouse. *If he really loves me, he would accept me for the way I look,* she reasoned. I had to help Joyce see that this is not what love is.

As we met week after week, Joyce shared with me that she had watched her mother and father fight over the very same issue. Joyce had reasoned that the apple had not fallen far from the tree, and that she would have the same weight struggles her mother battled. She admitted that once the comments began coming from Ben, she knew she was going to fight the same fight as her mother. What she did not realize was the subconscious punishment she was placing back on Ben. Her pain responded back through words and actions of punishment. Her thoughts were *You, too, must pay for my pain. You are partly responsible for this anyway. I have to stay home all day with these kids. It's enough to drive me to the kitchen ten times a day. And the fact that I always have food on the table when you get home each night should say a lot about my commitment to you. You are an unappreciative man and you don't deserve me. You have always been thin, and if I could go to the gym as much as you, I might be thin, too.* Word after word, Joyce was building a reservoir of pain that was sure to break at some point. The fact of the matter was that Joyce did not love herself. Her excuses were mounting up, and punishing Ben was only driving them further and further apart.

> When we **fixate** on negative self-talk and refuse to think **positively**, we see only doom and gloom ahead.

I remember the day Joyce walked into our coaching session a new woman. "I get it, Tammy. My issues are my issues. I cannot blame, punish, or expect another human being to make me completely happy outside of God."

Joyce then shared how she had played a scenario over and over in her mind as a young girl. Long before she married Ben, she had already accepted the fact that she would have a weight problem and had been internally processing responses. As a Life Coach I have seen this behavior time and time again. Clients often share with me that they have had certain fears from childhood that captivate their behavior as adults. Often the thoughts we rehearse in our head are:

- I will be fat.
- I will get a divorce.
- I will get cancer.
- My spouse will be unfaithful.
- I will not amount to anything.
- I will never have a healthy relationship.
- I will not be able to get pregnant.
- I will die at a young age.
- Someone I love will be in a horrible accident.
- I will always battle depression.

In Job 3:25 we read, "What I feared has come upon me; what I dreaded has happened to me" (NIV). When we fixate on negative self-talk and refuse to think positively, we see only doom and gloom ahead. Instead of considering what we can do to change our outlook, we transfer our anxieties and pain onto someone else. We blame or punish them for the things that go wrong in our lives, refusing to see our own agency. We all have issues, broken belief systems, hurts, flaws, and struggles. Pain transference is common in people who don't want to do their own personal work. When we own our personal behavior, we move into the place of repair and healing.

Pain transference is common in people who don't want to do their own personal work. When we own our personal behavior, we move into the place of repair & healing.

Joyce had seen the lies from her past and was ready to move into her true identity. Using punishment as a buffer to your pain will only boomerang back ten-fold. Replace the technique of punishment with self-responsibility and see God do a new work in your life.

PUNISHING OTHERS FOR BREAKING THE RULES

Don't we all desire to help the outcast, to care for the helpless and downtrodden, to give grace when not necessarily deserved? Well, maybe not, especially when it goes against our core belief system or personal conviction. When we see a co-worker staggering down the street late at night, clearly drunk, or when we learn of friends' affairs or deceit, our first reaction is often to judge them. Sometimes our judgment turns into punishment: We may lecture the person on how they should behave, or we may give that person the silent treatment until they repent of their wicked ways. We may send people packing on guilt trips, filling their suitcases with reminders of what they should have done and why they were wrong.

In working with people over the last thirty years I have witnessed several styles of punishment. We all assume the role of "setting society straight" at one time or another. We just use different means to achieve the same end. I have come up with five personalities of punishment that are often used to control another person. Read the list below and ask yourself which personality you have a tendency toward.

THE FIVE PERSONALITIES OF PUNISHMENT

The Policeman

This personality is looking for the bad guy day and night. You wear the badge of "law enforcer" and make it your goal to keep society straight. You live by the letter of the law and feel it is your obligation to point out misbehavior on anyone's part. You carry the rulebook for life in your back pocket and pull it out to read the chapter and verse when necessary. You feel you have always obeyed the law and you do not give grace often. Rules are meant to be followed, and "law enforcers" are meant to give citations.

The Mother

This personality hovers with the intention of training others up in righteousness. You see others as children incapable of making decisions on their own. Their bad behavior is a reflection on you so you play the guilt card to keep them in line. You know how to send people on an all-expenses-paid guilt trip vacation. You can be controlling with those you consider your children.

The Priest

This personality rules with absolute authority but will offer grace if the person is willing to confess and pay for their sin. That payment may be time spent together, formal apologies, or maybe even gifts. People respect you and your authority, but dread facing the confessional booth. Your words bring feelings of judgment and superiority. This approach brings guilt and embarrassment and is never a means to restoring a relationship.

The Watchdog

This personality feels it their responsibility to keep others safe. You are a watchdog and shadow. You take up an offence on others' behalf. When those you love have been hurt, it is your job to punish the offender. You have a hyper-sense of protection for them and will always defend their case. However, you are continuously telling them what to do and how to do it, stating it is for their own good. You use your bark and bite to remind others you are by their side. You are not beyond using ferocious growling to instill fear in others (and maybe in the ones you love). You believe it is in their best interest to allow you to protect them. This personality tends to be dominant and dictatorial.

The Silencer

This personality uses the silent treatment to ignore others. You use your emotions to step away from the offender and give them the cold shoulder. You want that person to feel the pressure of your displeasure in hopes that they will see the light and turn from their ways. Most people who use this type of punishment don't get over offenses quickly. You may even be looking for a way to vent some personal issue you're feeling and the people around you may have just gotten in the line of emotional fire.

As you can see, there are several approaches to punishing others for bad behavior. The question to ask yourself is, *Am I wasting time trying to punish others?* Punishment is an exhausting exercise that has the potential to hurt both parties involved.

Let's look at what God has to say about judging others. The story of the adulteress women caught by the religious leaders is one that has always intrigued me. In John 8 we read this account:

> Jesus went to the Mount of Olives. At dawn he appeared again in the temple courts, where all the people gathered around him, and he sat down to teach them.
>
> The teachers of the law and the Pharisees brought in a woman caught in adultery. They made her stand before the group and said to Jesus, "Teacher, this woman was caught in the act of adultery. In the Law Moses commanded us to stone such women. Now what do you say?" They were using this question as a trap, in order to have a basis for accusing him.
>
> But Jesus bent down and started to write on the ground with his finger. When they kept on questioning him, he straightened up and said to them, "If any one of you is without sin, let him be the first to throw a stone at her." Again he stooped down and wrote on the ground.
>
> At this, those who heard began to go away one at a time, the older ones first, until only Jesus was left, with the woman still standing there.
>
> Jesus straightened up and asked her, "Woman, where are they? Has no one condemned you?"
>
> "No one, sir," she said.
>
> "Then neither do I condemn you," Jesus declared. "Go now and leave your life of sin." *John 8:1-11 (NIV)*

Why is it that we look for ways to punish people we don't like or agree with? Why can't we take the higher road like Jesus and help someone quietly with his or her issues? Why not look for ways to help another human being move away from sin and struggle toward success? Why are we prone to look for the faults and shortcomings in a person before seeing their gifts and abilities? Why is there something that rises up in us that wants to make the guilty party pay for their transgressions?

I think we all know the answer to that question if we are to be honest. I want the world to run through my grid of truth, reality, and acceptance, and if that does not happen, then there will be consequences to pay. Punishment is our way of staying on top and staying in control. But it is not our job to punish or condemn people for their sins; God is the ultimate judge.

To be fair with the passage, Jesus was not condoning the woman's behavior. He looked at her straight in the eyes, (that in itself is enough to reckon with) and asked her an honest question. *"Woman, where are they? Has no one condemned you? ...Then neither do I condemn you, Go now and leave your life of sin."* He commands her to leave her life of sin, but first He tells her He does not condemn her.

We read in Romans 8:1, "There is now no condemnation for those who are in Christ Jesus" (NIV). Our Savior, Jesus Christ does not condemn. He does, however, correct and convict us to leave our lives of sin. There are definitely times of loving correction in relationships, but there are never times of condemning or aggressive punishment.

FOUR WAYS TO SKIP PUNISHMENT

1. Stop Fault-Finding

Look for what others do right, not wrong. You may need to recondition your mind to see the positive things others do, and with time, this can become a change in your lifestyle.

2. Get Over the Past

Often punishment toward another is over past hurt and pain. Until you let the past go, you will never be free to enjoy your future. You have the power to forgive and move on.

3. Be Patient

Most of us are in such a hurry that we don't even realize our irritation is coming from stress. We get angry and lose our temper, taking it out on the ones we love most, often punishing out of impatience. Stop and think before you speak. Is this really worth punishing someone for?

4. Unlock the Door

Self-punishment may be a response to feelings of guilt or regret. The choice to inflict self-pain can feel like we are paying for our choices. The reality is we are only prolonging the healing process. Grace and forgiveness are the keys to unlock the door of self-punishment.

A Woman of Influence skips punishment. She accepts God's grace and forgiveness and stops punishing herself. She accepts responsibility for her actions and does not shift blame onto others, punishing them. She recognizes she is not a policeman, mother, priest, watchdog, or a silencer. She is now free from using punishment as a means to correct, discipline, or instruct herself or those around her, and she instead relies on God for His healing, grace, and freedom.

We get angry and lose our temper,
taking it out on the ones
we **love** most, often **punishing**
out of impatience.

COACHING EXERCISE

In this coaching exercise I would like you to ask yourself some honest questions. The truth is no one wants to think they have a heart of punishment. But in reality we all at times want to control someone's actions and behaviors. As you read through the following questions, be honest with your answers.

1. Who are you most likely to punish for bad behavior and why?
   a. Self
   b. Friend
   c. Husband
   d. Child
   e. Parent
   f. Stranger

2. In what ways do you punish others?
   a. Issue citations
   b. Use guilt trips
   c. Require penance
   d. Instill fear
   e. Give the silent treatment

3. Reflect on a time you were punished for a bad decision. How did the punishment make you feel? Did using punishment help in any way?

   _____

   _____

   _____

   _____

   _____

   _____

COACHING EXERCISE

4. Reflect on a time you've punished someone else for a bad decision. How did the punishment make you feel? Make them feel? Did using punishment resolve the issue?

_____

_____

_____

_____

_____

_____

FOOTNOTES

[8] Understanding self-harm. (2014). *Psychology Today*. Retrieved from http://www.psychologytoday.com/basics/self-harm

JUMP INTO YOUR FUTURE

jump (verb): To move suddenly and quickly in a specified way.

A **Woman of Influence**

has made up her mind to take calculated risks,
and does not fear her future.

*"The sparrows jumped before they knew how to fly,
and they learned to fly only because they had jumped."*

Lauren Oliver

HAVE A PLAN

plan (noun): A scheme, program, or method worked out beforehand for the accomplishment of an objective.

The heart of man plans his way, but the Lord establishes his steps.
Proverbs 16:9 (ESV)

I can jump from one idea to another faster than a five-legged frog. Some call it the curse of an idea-list (rather than an idealist). I have lists and lists of ideas—all over my desk, in my purse, in my car, in my briefcase, even in my kitchen cabinet. One day as I sat with my cup of coffee, I decided to gather up all my great ideas and see where they had gotten me: *book titles, t-shirt designs, gadgets, ministries, blogs, fitness routines, reality shows, and so much more.* I thought about the impact these great ideas could make on so many lives. But that was all they were—ideas cased in dreams.

Ideas are wonderful, unless all you do is make list upon list and never do anything with them. Ideas can be nothing more than a distraction if you don't have a plan of action, so in this chapter I will share with you, step by step, how to turn an idea into a reality. A Woman of Influence moves forward into her future with plans, and accomplishing those plans can look different for each of us. However, there are three basic steps: First, we need to accept the challenge to move into our divine destiny. Next, we need to take uncomfortable risks. Finally, we need to focus on discipline to stay on course and see the dreams become reality. Ladies, get your sneakers on because we are getting ready to jump into our futures.

ACCEPT THE CHALLENGE

Over the years I have met with hundreds of women who have a desire to do something great with their lives, but never seem to be able to push past the barrier of fear and doubt. Kelly was such a woman.

I'll never forget the day Kelly and I met for her first coaching session. We had emailed back and forth a few times before she could muster up the courage to finally meet with me. By her own admission, she needed help with coming out of her crippling fear and personal timidity.

I had made it to our meeting location a few minutes early, so I pulled out my laptop to do some work. As each woman walked through the door I would lift my head to make eye contact, and then determine if that was my client. I had never met Kelly before, but she reassured me she had been to my website and knew what I looked like, so it would not be an issue. Five minutes past the hour, then ten, finally fifteen minutes later, I texted Kelly to see if she was still coming. To my surprise she texted back, "I am here."

"Where?" I texted.

"Standing right next to you."

I looked up and saw a beautiful woman standing next to me smiling. "Are you Kelly?" I asked.

"Yes."

"Why didn't you tell me you were here?"

"I didn't want to bother you."

That's when I knew we had some work to do. Kelly was beyond timid. She was frozen. As I sat and listened to her story, I realized Kelly had been a victim of an overbearing father. Her dad had not only been physically abusive to her, but emotionally abusive as well. Any time Kelly would say something with the slightest hint of confidence, her father would knock her upside the head and tell her to watch her mouth. She was told she would not amount to anything and the only thing she had going for her was her good looks. She was told she would need her good looks for a man to ever notice her.

Kelly was a broken, fragile young woman who had more going for her than she could ever imagine. Her eyes were kind and she had a smile that was infectious. If we could only learn to see what we have, not just what we don't have, I thought.

The first step for Kelly moving forward was to believe she *could* move forward, that her past was just that—her past—that God had created a plan for her life and that she could succeed. In Jeremiah 29:11 it says, "I know the plans I have for you, declares the Lord, plans to prosper you and not to harm you, plans to give you hope and a future" *(NIV)*. Once Kelly could see that she was a new creation in Christ and the old things of her life were gone, she would then be free to move forward. In II Corinthians 5:17 we read, "Therefore, if anyone is in Christ, he is a new creation; old things have passed away; behold, all things have become new" (KJV).

Get your **sneakers** on because we are getting **ready to jump** into our futures.

Step by step, Kelly started to write out her story. She was now ready to take responsibility for her actions and decisions. No person or problem could keep her from the plans God had for her. Kelly accepted the challenges before her and was ready to put her sneakers on and jump into her future.

TAKE AN UNCOMFORTABLE RISK

Having a plan and following God can mean taking uncomfortable risks. For some, these risks may be emotional, like forgiving someone or choosing to trust again. For others, the risks may be more tangible, like starting a business or moving to a new city. A woman from the Old Testament took great risks in seeking out God and His protection. Her name is Rahab, and she was a prostitute.

I believe Rahab was looking for God when the two spies of Israel knocked on her door. As the adage goes, "When the pupil is ready, the teacher will appear." Rahab was ready to take a risk and put her future in the hands of a loving God who knew her heart.

I cannot imagine how much courage it took for Rahab to trust men, let alone two foreigners. It was a time of war, and Rahab let them into her home to hide. These two men wanted nothing more than a place to lodge and reasoned that the home of a harlot was as good as any for strange men to show up. Rahab told the two men to go upstairs and she hid them safely before they could be found. She then lied to the governing authorities on their behalf and sent the authorities on a wild goose chase looking in the wrong direction. This woman just might be my hero.

I think when you finally reach the point of no turning back, you are at the best spot in the world. The only way to go is forward. Rahab then told the two spies that she had heard of them and their God and wanted the power they had. She had heard how Jehovah God had protected them and had promised them her land. She then made a bold request:

> Now then, please swear to me by the Lord that you will show kindness to my family, because I have shown kindness to you. Give me a sure sign that you will spare the lives of my father and mother, my brothers and sisters, and all who belong to them—and that you will save us from death. "Our lives for your lives!" the men assured her. "If you don't tell what we are doing, we will treat you kindly and faithfully when the Lord gives us the land. *Joshua 2:12-14 (NIV)*

Rahab certainly qualifies as someone willing to take an uncomfortable risk. You cannot jump into your future without taking some risk, and God will be there for you as you take that risk. Not only did the two spies keep their word to protect and preserve Rahab and her family, but she also went on to be in the direct lineage of Jesus Christ. When you step forward to take a risk, consider these encouraging words from the book of Joshua: "Have I not commanded you? Be strong and courageous. Do not be afraid; do not be discouraged, for the LORD your God will be with you wherever you go" *Joshua 1:9 (NIV)*.

FOCUS ON DISCIPLINE

Having a plan is insufficient if you lack the most important ingredient: discipline. A Woman of Influence focuses on what is necessary to keep moving forward and trusts God to show her the path ahead. After working with Annette, I made a questionnaire to gauge the level of commitment that each client is willing to extend in our time together; discipline is essential for staying on track and moving forward.

Annette was a stay-at-home mother of four. Although she loved the opportunity to be home with her kids, she was itching to do something new and creative with her life. Her babies were growing up, and with the youngest going into middle school Annette was getting antsy.

Her closest friend, Patty, was a successful makeup consultant who had gone from saleswoman to an executive in the company. She would host home parties as well as executive training courses to numerous businesses in the area. When they were out together, Annette was always amazed at the number of people who knew Patty and how they would thank her for helping them feel more beautiful.

Until you are **ready to run** the race, there is no use putting on the shoes.

"Patty, you seem to love what you do," Annette would say each time they were together. "What a privilege it must be to have people personally thank you for what you do." Patty would always agree that what she did brought value and joy to those she worked with and that she couldn't see herself doing anything other than being a beauty consultant.

Annette took Patty's example to heart and decided it was time to make some changes in her own life. *But what can I do?* Annette reasoned. *I have not gone to college. I don't know what skills I have, and I still have four children at home.* That's when Annette turned to coaching for help.

Annette was off to a great start. She was determined to assess her life and develop a plan for her future. The first several sessions Annette was on board. She was enjoying the process and personal self-discovery. But over a period of time, Annette began making excuses for her late assignments and tardy appointments, which showed me that she did not have the discipline needed to move forward.

The *lack of discipline*

will keep you from your divine destiny.

One thing I do as a Life Coach is explain to my clients that this process is not about me. When a client comes to me for coaching, I always start with a questionnaire: Are You Coachable? And Annette was the very reason I created the questionnaire. She lacked commitment. As much as Annette aspired to be like Patty, she was not willing to put forth the effort. Until you are ready to run the race, there is no use putting on the shoes. The lack of discipline and focus will keep you from moving into your divine destiny.

JUMP INTO YOUR FUTURE

Whether you relate to Kelly, Rahab, or Annette, one thing is for sure: These women had to jump into their future. Are you ready to do the same? There are four steps to follow when developing plans for your future. These plans could be personal projects, relational goals, spiritual endeavors—anything big or small that contributes to becoming a Woman of Influence, a woman who seeks after God's plans for her life. These four steps have been proven time and time again with numerous clients throughout my practice.

WRITE IT DOWN

When you first get an idea for a project, write it down. The best way I know to develop an idea is to ask the reporter's questions, *Who, What, When, Where, Why, and How*:

WHO will be involved in or affected by the project?

_____

_____

_____

_____

WHAT items, skills, materials, etc. will you need for the project?

_____

_____

_____

_____

WHEN will the project be complete?

_____

_____

_____

_____

WHERE will this project take you?

_____

_____

_____

_____

WHY is this project important to you or to others?

_____

_____

_____

_____

HOW will you evaluate your success?

_____

_____

_____

_____

After answering these questions you will be ready to articulate your future. Writing down your thoughts will not only help you visualize the plan, it will help you process your steps.

TRY IT ON

Not every idea or goal is right for you. Let me explain. One day I saw the cutest girl in a pair of Rock & Republic jeans—you know, the cute blue jeans with the R's on the back pockets. Well, I thought I just had to have a pair. I mean, they fit that girl like a glove. So off to the mall I went. With the assistance of the sales clerk, I grabbed a pair of jeans and flew into the dressing room. Slipping one leg in after the other, I pulled them up, only to be greatly disappointed. They did not look on me anything like they did on the young girl I saw earlier. They were not made to fit me.

You see, those jeans are made for tall, slim ladies, not average, athletic bodies. They were not made for me. Fortunately, the sweet sales clerk saw the disappointment on my face and offered a solution. Having already sized me up, she knew just what brands were made for my personal body type. She said, "I think I have the perfect brand for you. After she assessed me correctly, I left that day with a pair of jeans I have worn out and since bought several additional pairs of.

Not every idea is right for you any more than any pair of jeans is made to fit you. You must assess your plan in the very beginning stages by asking yourself a few questions:

- Does this fit me?
- Can I commit to what it takes?
- Do I have the necessary tools and skills, or can I find someone who does and who will help me?

ASK AROUND

It is important that you get an honest opinion from family, friends, and colleagues. Ask them to be objective in answering the following questions:

- Do you think I have the skillset for this project?
- Can you see my passion lasting for this idea?
- Do you think it fits my personality?

Remember these tips:

- Smart people put smarter people around them.
- Smart people ask the right questions.
- Smart people hear the truth.
- Smart people don't make excuses.

CREATE YOUR FOCUS CARD

You can't get started on your plan until you are able to write it down, try it on, and get a confirmation from those who know you best. Then you are ready to move into the final phase, which is to create your Focus Card. A Focus Card is the best plan I know to produce results. It will ask the right questions while holding you accountable to deadlines.

I use this exercise often to keep myself focused and accountable for all sorts of ideas, goals, and endeavors. Some people with whom I've used the Focus Card have focused on a task or a personal goal, like organization or budgeting. One co-worker chose something as simple as smiling more often. Others have used it to challenge themselves to argue less or to trust more.

I recently used a Focus Card to plan an upcoming event I would be leading. Our Women of Influence NEW Conference was quickly approaching in January, and I didn't want to wait until the last minute to begin planning. I knew I wanted to combine a concert with the conference, which would take us to a whole new level. I also knew that artists book up fast, so if I wanted to have an A-list artist, I would need to book early.

Another area of planning I was concerned with was the venue. I believed that God had given me a vision for the NEW Conference with thousands of women, but was this the year? It was only our second year hosting the conference and we were a new organization to the community. I thought the best thing to do was to set a numerical goal and then work the numbers.

Having hundreds of women our first year, I felt safe in doubling the number of women who would attend the second year. Next on the list was the venue. Our church had hosted the first conference and we had ample room, but to double our number we would have to rethink the set-up.

Taking a step of faith, I made an appointment with a conference center in the area. It was beautiful and perfectly suited for our needs, but it was expensive. I knew we could not afford a premium artist, a keynote speaker, and an off-site venue.

This is where planning comes in. It does not matter what your idea is, there are certain steps you must take. I had already passed through the steps of write it down, try it on, and ask around, so we were ready to plan it out. After meeting with the committee for feedback, we decided to use our current location for one more year. Once the decision was made, we were free to start planning the event. The Focus Card was a great tool to keep me on track. As I processed through my action steps, I knew just where I was going. I utilized my advocates to get things accomplished, kept my eye on what to avoid, and stayed away from the things that drained my attention.

Jumping into your future is fun, but it will take some work, and the Focus Card is a vehicle to keep you on track. I use the Card on a regular basis for both decision-making and personal development. In the Coaching Exercise, I will walk you through how to make your own.

The **Focus Card** was a great tool
to keep me on track. As I processed through my
action steps, I knew just where I was going.
I utilized my advocates to get things
accomplished, kept my eye on what to
avoid, and stayed away from the things
that drained my attention.

COACHING EXERCISE

1. Get a 3×5 or 4×6 piece of cardstock. On one side write in large letters the one word or phrase that describes what you want your Focus to be (your project) for the next thirty days. This can be an event you are planning, a goal you have set, a project you need to complete, or an attribute you need to work on.

2. Now on the back draw a line horizontally across the card and vertically down the card, to make four sections.

   a. On the upper left corner write **ACTION**.
      List three steps you can take in the next thirty days.

   b. On the upper right corner write **ADVOCATE**.
      List three people who can help you succeed in the next thirty days.

   c. On the lower left corner write **AVOID**.
      List three things you might need to avoid in order to succeed.

   d. On the lower right corner write **ATTENTION**.
      List three things that are distracting your attention.

	Action	Advocate
TASK		
	Avoid	Attention

Front   Back

A Focus Card is key for your success.

EXERCISE FAITH

faith (noun): Belief that does not rest on logical proof or material evidence; the theological virtue defined as secure belief in God and a trusting acceptance of God's will.

Now faith is the assurance of things hoped for, the conviction of things not seen. *Hebrews 11:1 (ESV)*

Say it so... and see it done.

After you have the plan written out, it is time to move into the realm of faith. One of the hardest parts of having plans and moving into the future is the uncertainty and the lack of control. A Woman of Influence must surrender control to God and exercise her faith to see dreams and ideas become reality.

THE MEANING OF **FAITH**

Living in America, many of us grew up with a sense of faith —the kind of faith that says there is a God who cares for the world and holds all the pieces together. Faith was something we heard and believed in, mostly in some sort of hopeful way. People most frequently come face to face with faith when we're holding our breath and praying things will turn out OK.

My first experience exercising faith was while I was in the hospital giving birth to my first son. I had just transitioned into my last big contraction as he made his way into this world, when no sooner the nurse whisked him off to the ICU. I was told his lungs had collapsed and he was in critical condition.

My heart broke as I laid in the recovery room wondering if I would ever see my son's face again. Hours passed as nurse after nurse came in to check on me. They told me if he made it through the night they would allow me see him the next day, but they were not hopeful he would make it.

I remember crying out to God to save my son. Promises were made to be a better person, to read my Bible more, be a good wife—all the things we say when we are negotiating with God.

Soon after bargaining with God I grew silent; I just lay still, hoping He would speak to me, that He would give me some reassurance that my son would live and that he would be fine.

The room was quiet and my heart was still for the first time in hours. Then He spoke. Faith is believing something is so, when it is not so, in order for it to be so. I love the way God uses words, scripture, events, and people to speak to us.

Faith is ***believing*** something is so, when it is not so, in order for it to be so.

A few months before my son was born, I began working through a morning devotional on faith. It was actually called *Faith Workbook* by Manley Beasley. My husband and I had become friends with Manley through a mutual acquaintance, and he had begun discipling us in our faith.

One day Manley looked at me and said, "Tammy, faith is believing something is so, when it's not so, in order for it to be so."

Now, I had grown up in the church and thought I knew a lot about God, but that statement made no earthly sense to me. I was having trouble repeating it, let alone grasping it. How could something be so when it is not? I took the workbook morning by morning, reading page after page. This faith concept is complicated. I was not sure how to even go about understanding the definition, let alone conceiving its truth.

I remember finishing the workbook wondering if I would ever understand the meaning of faith. As a child, I had put my trust in Jesus Christ to save my life, but that involved belief. Yes, I believed Jesus loved me and died for my sin. I believed He rose from the grave and went to heaven where He has prepared a place for me forever. As a child that simple faith saved my eternal life. But this was different. How do you believe something is so when it is not?

Manley Beasley's definition of faith kept ringing over and over in my mind. In the hospital I knew it was God speaking to me because I had not been able to even memorize Manley's definition of faith. If anything, I kept mixing the words up in my head. But that day they were crystal clear.

Tammy, you have to believe it is so, when it is not so, in order for it to be so.

"What are you saying God?" I asked. "Are you speaking to me?"

Yes, I am asking if you are ready to experience faith. Are you ready to move into the divine realm of My Spirit and see mountains move? That is what faith is, Tammy. Mountains move.

I remembered the verse I had memorized as a little girl: "If you have faith as small as a mustard seed, you can say to this mountain, "Move from here to there," and it will move. Nothing will be impossible for you" Matthew 17:20 (NIV).

God spoke to my heart and said that fear was a mountain, that the nurse's report was a mountain, that my lack of belief was a mountain. God's Spirit gently moved in the recovery room and spoke to my heart.

Do you want to understand faith, Tammy?

"Yes," I cried in my heart.

Then simply believe Me. Say your son will live, even though the doctors say he will not, and your faith in Me wills it so.

For the first time I understood faith. It was more than head knowledge of truth. It was releasing my understanding to the power of the all-knowing God of the universe. It was my faith (believing it so) in the God who gives life that made it so.

Today my son is a strong successful banker with a beautiful family of his own. I believe God used my son to teach me a great lesson in faith.

TESTS OF **FAITH**

My faith journey has grown over the years as I have stepped out and asked God to move mountains in my life. I do not receive everything I ask of Him. Sometimes the mountains are there longer than I like; some still haven't moved. But I still exercise my faith and wait for His answer.

Not long ago I was asked to meet with a mother who had just gone through a horrific situation with her child. A car accident nearly took her son's life and left him physically challenged.

As mothers we vow to keep our children safe and dream of them becoming happy adults with families of their own. This was not going to be the case for my new friend. As we talked, she began to share her faith journey and spiritual experience with God. Growing up in a religious home, she had been taught to be a good person and to try to meet the needs of those less fortunate. She had a good marriage, successful business, and two great kids. Life was right on track, or so it seemed.

However, accidents, setbacks, and difficulties test our faith. It is very easy to talk about God when things are going well, but just try keeping your faith foremost when trying to make sense of tragedy and loss. While sitting with Sue I realized her struggle was not only the tragedy of her son, but also her personal struggle with her faith. She began to share with me the difficulty of staying positive. Thoughts, questions, and memories were bombarding her mind right and left. "I want to have faith," she exclaimed. "I'm just exhausted from my negative thoughts and memories."

Crisis and loss will test our faith every time. Our mind and emotions lead us down a trail of anger, doubt, and fear. The thought of faith seems too big to entertain. As I sat with Sue that day, I knew we had to start with her mind, then her emotions and faith would follow.

Her difficulties had caused her to wonder if God was trying to get her attention. Had her lack of commitment caused this tragedy to happen? Negative thoughts like this bombard our minds when we are in crisis. *Could I have done something to stop this from happening? Should I have been more involved in my child's life? Were there signs I missed along the way?* The list goes on and on as we reason what could have been done to prevent the tragedy.

But these are simply isolated thoughts that try to control our minds in the process of crisis. The key is to stop these thoughts from taking over your mind. Trying to fix the outcome of a crisis is like trying to put baking power in a cake after it comes out of the oven…It's already done. To exercise faith is to assume God wants the best for you and is willing to act on your behalf. The battlefield is in the mind and this is where the war must be fought. I had to help Sue understand in her mind that God still loves her and she had not done anything wrong to cause the accident. As much as she wanted to believe God could heal her son, she still had to go through the process of questioning to get there.

To **exercise faith** is to assume God wants the best for you and is willing to act on your behalf. The **battlefield** is in the **mind** and this is where the war must be fought.

Sue's story is not unlike so many others I hear. We even find a similar story in the Bible of two sisters who questioned God's timing in their lives. In John 11 we read the story of Mary and Martha asking Jesus to come quickly because their brother was sick. Now this was not just any request. Their brother Lazarus was a good friend of the Messiah. Jesus had frequently been in their home and ministered to their community. Mary had anointed Jesus with expensive oil and wiped His feet with her hair. They were friends, good friends. They had watched Jesus heal many people along the way, even some who did not deserve it. So when the need arose for the Master to come quickly and heal their brother, the thought never entered their minds that there would be an issue. Their faith was in the fact that He could, not whether or not He would. Day after day passed and still, no Jesus. Lazarus was getting worse as the days passed until finally he took his last breath. *How could this happen,* the sisters reasoned. *We are friends of the Master. We are not some random people asking for help. We have done so much to assist with His ministry. How could He do this to us?* The worst part was that Jesus knew their brother was sick, and He didn't even try to hurry and come.

This is when faith wanes—when you trust that God can, and He doesn't. Once again the warfare takes place in your mind. Do you still trust God is all-loving and kind when your circumstances say otherwise? This is precisely where Mary and Martha found themselves—trusting Jesus on the other side of a crisis. What I love about reading this story is I can see the end result. Jesus had a plan, and everyone would benefit from the lesson. Upon arriving at the home of Mary and Martha, Jesus was met with hurt, questions, and anger. (Much like you and I when we don't like the outcome of our situations.) *Where were you? How could you allow this to happen? You are the Master of the Universe and have the power to make things right.* Jesus allowed Martha to voice her thoughts and then began to walk her down the path of the Divine. The truth about any crisis is it has the potential to make or break your future destiny.

Once you have exhausted all your reasoning, you simply step into the realm of faith with the Father, letting go of all your assumptions and trusting **God's perfect plan** for your life.

When difficulty arises we question why God allowed the situation to happen in the first place. We process through our deeds and actions hoping to convince God that we deserve His help. We know the crisis is too big for us alone and we ultimately need His support and guidance, but we are not quite sure if He will come through.

This is the perfect place to begin to exercise your faith. When the outcome needed is bigger than your ability, you are ready to move into the faith realm.

After I spent several hours with Sue, she began to understand that she must take control of her thoughts and emotions. Faith is an exercise that comes with time and supernatural understanding. Once you have exhausted all your reasoning, you simply step into the realm of faith with the Father, letting go of all your assumptions and trusting God's perfect plan for your life.

STEPS OF FAITH

Let me share with you five steps that can assist you on the journey of faith. Faith does not happen over night. It is a process of thinking, believing, and eventually embracing the arms of a loving God. As you read through these steps, ask yourself where you are on the journey. You may take longer on one step than another. You may even go backwards at times. That is OK. It is all part of the journey of faith. My prayer is that the Holy Spirit will comfort and speak to you along the way.

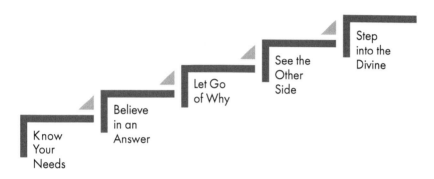

Know you have a need.

Mary and Martha had lost their brother. The death of Lazarus had left both sisters asking hard questions about Jesus. The death of a loved one leaves a void like no other in our hearts. I have experienced family members and close friends passing away. The need for answers and comfort are equal in the process. The first step of faith is knowing you have a need.

Believe in an answer.

Jesus could have healed Lazarus if He chose to. Many people get stuck on this step because they are too angry to see the answer. They argue it should not have happened in the first place so why believe there is an answer. Hope is the key to unlock this door of thinking. Mary and Martha knew even though Lazarus was gone, Jesus still had the power to heal.

Let go of the why.

Mary and Martha's relationship, friendship, and good works were
not enough to save their brother. Both sisters struggled with the "why" of
Lazarus' death. We even read in the story that the people of the town were
amazed at how much Jesus loved Lazarus, yet He was nowhere to be found
throughout his sickness. Someone once asked me after losing a loved one,
"How long will I grieve like this?" "As long as you need to," I answered. Until
you have exhausted all your means of thought and emotion, you are not
ready to move on. And that is OK. Jesus meets us when we are ready, and He
knows just when that is.

Jesus meets us **when we are ready**,
and He knows just when that is.

See the other side.

Jesus asked Martha if she could see Lazarus alive again. When you are
ready to move from the physical to the spiritual realm, you will see the
Divine. It must be seen in the spiritual before it can be experienced. Jesus
knew Mary and Martha had seen a lot of miracles. Now He wanted them to
experience one. There are so many wonderful parts of this story, but one in
particular is that Jesus is walking the faith journey step by step with each
sister. He is helping them see into the divine realm—something that they
may have not experienced without the death of Lazarus.

Step into the divine.

"Unbind him and let him go" *(John 11:43, ESV)*. This is one of my
favorite statements in the Bible. Not until you are loosed from the bonds that
trap you can you be free to see what God sees. I believe many today are
bound in burial garments and are blind to the things of God. When Jesus
spoke to Lazarus to "Come forth," He spoke with authority in the spiritual
realm. God desires each of us to step into the Divine and walk out of our
burial clothes.

OBSTACLES TO **SUCCESS**

We all face obstacles and setbacks in life—that is to be expected. The key is to be prepared and have a plan to overcome the things that block you from succeeding. Faith is one of the keys to your success. Big dreams and opportunities can only truly be seen through the eyes of faith.

Making a Focus Card is not enough if you lack faith. I'll bet your mind has already come up with ways and reasons your Focus Card won't work. For example, there were many obstacles for me to overcome in planning the NEW Conference. I could have allowed the mountain of excuses to keep me from proceeding, or I could take them one at a time, and by prayer, through faith, see them become a reality. When I look at the front of my Focus Card I see: NEW Conference. A few of my obstacles might be: I don't have enough staff; I need more money; and I don't know how I will advertise.

Working with women on their Focus Cards, I have heard many obstacles for success.

- I don't have the time.
- I don't have the money.
- I'm afraid.
- I'm too lazy.
- It's too big of a risk.
- What if I lack the skill?
- I tend to procrastinate.
- What if I fail?

All of these obstacles are keys to unlock your faith. Each obstacle is an opportunity to go to God in prayer. For example, with the obstacle of staff, I pray, *God, bring me skilled, focused women who want to be a part of a powerful women's movement.* With the obstacle of money, I ask, *God, show me unique ways to raise funds for the NEW Conference.* For my needs in advertising, I request, *God, direct me to those who can help advertise the Conference.*

Until you step out into the realm of risk you will never see the supernatural in your life. A Woman of Influence must learn to exercise her faith in the realm of the supernatural. She must be stretched beyond her personal capability and move into the vision God sees for her life.

COACHING EXERCISE

To see your Focus Card become a reality, you must exercise faith. You believe there is a Divine element working on your behalf to bring about your success. God is our Creator and has given each of us the ability to be creative. The Focus Card is simply a way to keep you on track with your goals and plans. Keep in mind your Focus word can be something personal like: "Smile More" or "Rest" or something task-oriented like: "Get Organized" or "Build Business." The purpose is to stay focused on one word for thirty days as you begin to build structure into your goal.

1. Take out your Focus Card. Looking at the word on the front of your card, list three obstacles keeping you from success.

_____

_____

_____

_____

_____

_____

2. Now write a prayer, sentence, or declaration of faith that overshadows each obstacle.

_____

_____

_____

_____

_____

_____

COACHING EXERCISE

3. Ask God to reveal areas that are keeping you from trusting Him
    completely.

    _____

    _____

    _____

    _____

    _____

    _____

4. List at least one person with whom to share the end results of your
    Focus Card.

    _____

    _____

    _____

    _____

    _____

    _____

CHAPTER SIX

ENJOY THE JOURNEY

enjoy (verb): to receive pleasure or satisfaction from; to have the use or benefit of.

This is the day the Lord has made, let us rejoice and be glad in it.
Psalm 118:24 (ESV)

It has been said, "If you have one eye on yesterday, and one eye on tomorrow, you're going to be cockeyed today."

Author Unknown

In working through these chapters, you have been on a journey towards becoming a Woman of Influence. Each time you have chosen to skip entitlement, resentment, and punishment, you have taken strides toward a life of fulfillment and joy. As you identify goals and plans and take steps of faith, God is leading you toward your destiny. The journey into your future with God will both bless and stretch you beyond your wildest dreams.

Part of jumping into your future is learning to embrace each day to the fullest. The art of embracing the moment is one that takes time and concentration. In the fast-paced culture we live in, it has become hard to slow down and appreciate the moment. We are conditioned to run fast and think ahead. Taking the time to enjoy the journey means letting all distractions go. It is taking note of what you do have, not what you don't have. It's counting your blessings, not your problems. A Woman of Influence trusts God's plans for her future and enjoys the journey, living life to the fullest in the present, yet knowing when to reflect upon what she has overcome and when to look ahead and consider the future.

EMBRACE THE JOURNEY

In the book of Ruth we read about a woman who chose to leave her past behind and trust in God to provide for her future. Ruth embraced the journey and lived one day at a time, but the path was not easy, and the destination was not always clear. Each time I read this account it causes me to ask myself, *Would I have been that confident in the face of difficulty and uncertainty?*

The story is set in a time of drought and despair for Israel. Many Israelites, including Naomi, Elimelech, and their two sons, had moved to nearby Moab to escape the drought. Ruth was a Moabite, and she married one of these sons. After ten years of marriage, her life seemed to be predictable and routine, but things changed when her father-in-law passed away, followed by her husband and her brother-in-law. In a matter of moments, Naomi, Ruth, and her sister-in-law faced a difficult decision of how to survive as widows.

By then the drought had come to an end in Judea, and Naomi decided to make her way back home to be with friends and family. She called her daughters-in-law to her side, sharing her decision with them both: "You have been by my side through the most difficult time of my life. You are both near and dear to my heart, but now it is time to go our separate ways. This is your home and your people. Your only hope for a future is to go back to your family and start life over again."

Both girls wept bitterly at the very thought of saying goodbye to Naomi, but her words were strong. Embracing her and weeping, one daughter-in-law said goodbye and turned to walk away. But Ruth would not concede, nor would she leave. She recognized that a difficult journey lay ahead, but she wanted to share it with Naomi and her God. Choosing to put the past behind her, Ruth uttered the words that have impacted both history and current culture alike:

> Don't urge me to leave you or to turn back from you. Where you go I will go, and where you stay I will stay. Your people will be my people and your God my God. Where you die I will die, and there I will be buried. May the Lord deal with me, be it ever so severely, if even death separates you and me. *Ruth 1:16-17 (NIV)*

Ruth's journey was just beginning, and each day she had to choose to move forward. Arriving back home brought brokenness and pain to Naomi's heart. Friends and relatives anxiously came to greet the women with open arms. The reunion was not what Naomi had expected. Full of emotion and memory, Naomi had a meltdown and became very bitter as she allowed herself to experience the pain from her loss. Seeing her brokenness, Ruth gently helped her up and sought refuge for the two of them.

Now, it was the beginning of barley season, and Ruth knew she had to make a living to care for herself and her mother-in-law. Little did Ruth know God was preparing the way for her step by step. Quietly making her way through the fields of leftovers, Ruth was spotted by a man named Boaz. This was not just any man (it never is when God is in the story); he was a relative of her father-in-law. Word had gotten out how deeply Ruth cared for her mother-in-law and how she worked selflessly to get her back to Bethlehem with her family.

The **journey** into your future with God
will both bless and stretch you
beyond *your* **wildest dreams.**

Boaz began making exceptions for Ruth in the fields and saw that she got a little extra barley along the way. Naomi recognized that this attention from Boaz was God's hand in Ruth's life, and it reawakened her spirit. Naomi directed Ruth in the proper ways to respond to Boaz's attention. As was God's plan, he fell in love with her, and courted her with the purest of intentions. Ruth and Boaz married, and they had a son named Obed, which made Ruth the great-grandmother of King David and in the direct lineage of the Messiah.

When Ruth set out alongside Naomi on their journey back to Judea, she was embracing a larger journey—God's destiny for her life. The path was unpredictable and difficult, and each day she had to choose to move forward, to put the pain of loss behind her. She chose to take care of herself and her mother-in-law, and to trust that God would take care of them both.

Funny thing about the journey of life…it never looks like we think it should, and the destination is almost never in sight. Ruth was no exception, but she was willing to continue walking in spite of her fears. None of us can be certain what our journeys will look like down the road. We can plan, pray, and try to prepare, but in reality, it is God who knows our destiny.

Many are the plans in a person's heart, but it is the Lord's purpose that prevails. *Proverbs 19:21 (NIV)*

BE STILL

As we move forward on our journeys, we can get caught up in distractions. Some of us, like Naomi, struggle with moving forward because the pain of the past captures our attention. Others are so busy thinking about the destination that they forget the joy is in the journey. I know I get so caught up with daily demands that I can miss out on the sweet moments of life. One day as I sat in my chair asking God what He wanted me to do, His presence became so real to me. I sat quietly meditating on God. I heard Him speak to my heart. *Be still…*

Silence came over me like a calm river waiting for the morning sun to rise. I sat still for sometime before I asked God, "What next?"

Be still, My child, I heard His voice whisper.

I must admit, I struggled to sit still and concentrate on the voice of God. At first I heard the air conditioner, the refrigerator, the dog next door; I even heard my stomach growl. What is it about silence that makes everything else seem so loud? Once again I tried to clear my thoughts. "Ok God, here I am. What do you want to say to me?"

Shhhh, be still.

I sat still for sometime before God came to me again. I heard my heart beating and then the voice of God gently spoke.

Open the door.

As I sat with my eyes closed, I saw a door open in my heart.

Walk through the door, My child.

As I passed through the door, it was as though I entered my childhood. I saw myself with pigtails riding my bike. I saw my backyard and my bedroom. I saw my schoolteachers and then my sisters laughing. I saw good times and painful times. Memories both good and bad were before my eyes. Then the door shut as I sat in silence. Moments later another door opened. As I walked through the door I saw my marriage. I saw the love I have for my husband and the good times we have shared together. I saw his sweet smile and the intimate secrets we have shared. I saw the pain I have caused him and the times I was not my best self. I also saw the hurt he has caused me and the times of loneliness I have experienced. As I sat reflecting, the door shut. While processing my memories, I saw a third door open. Without hesitation I walked in. This was the door to my children. I found myself smiling at their baby pictures, laughing at their silly stunts, and enjoying our times as a family. Then I saw hurt—the hurt I have caused them and the hurt they have caused me. My heart was heavy, yet tender for the love I felt for each of my children. Stillness was all around me. I was quiet and God was quiet. Then without warning, the final door opened. As I approached, I wondered what more God had to show me. Walking through the door, I was curious about where He would take me now.

This is your future, I felt Him say to my heart. *This is what I have planned for you if you are willing to trust Me.*

Step by step He introduced me to each path and hillside He had arranged for my future. I saw visions and dreams I had only hoped for up to this point. Now God was asking me to trust His perfect will for my life. As I took a deep breath, the door closed. I sat still and motionless for a moment.

"What now, God? What are you saying?"

I heard a still, small voice say, *And know that I am God.*

I asked, "Is that all?"

God said, *Be still, and know that I am God.*

That experience transformed my life forever. Even as I recount the details, I am moved to intimacy with God. When we allow ourselves to get caught up in the details, we miss out on the supernatural experience God is waiting to show us. As we learn to slow down and receive the gifts of God, we begin to enjoy the journey day by day.

Others are so busy thinking
about the destination that they forget
the **joy** is in the **journey.**

I have developed a coaching concept called "The Present is Perfect." This applies to our life journeys because being stuck in the memories of the past or fixating on details for the future prevent us from being still and knowing He is God.

THE PRESENT IS PERFECT

The mind has three time zones—the past, the present, and the future. Our minds can only retain one thought at a time, so we determine which mind-zone we want to be in. If you are like most of my clients, you are either stuck in how to process your past or you are dreaming how to improve your future. The problem is that you are missing the most important time of your life. TODAY!

There are several reasons we live in the mind-zones of the past and the future. Let's explore why we spend so much time there.

LIVING IN THE PAST?

Life as a Victim

Since being a victim is subjective, no one can challenge or refute your feelings. It is your experience and your supposition; therefore, it is true. However, just because you feel it and can justify it does not mean it is all true. When you choose to be a victim, the past becomes a planet with its own gravitational pull, and you just orbit around it, reliving the experiences and feelings that hurt you. But you can choose to be a survivor, not a victim. A survivor acknowledges the pain of the past but chooses to live today with hope for the future.

I took you from the ends of the earth, from its farthest corners I called you. I said 'You are my servant'; I have chosen you and have not rejected you. So do not fear, for I am with you, do not be dismayed, for I am your God. I will strengthen you and help you. I will uphold you with my righteous right hand.

Isaiah 41:9-10 (NIV)

Life as the Hero

If you've had a successful past, it is a safe and glorious place to live. You can relive your successes every time you tell the stories again. The stories are your "life fuel" that give you significance and personal worth. To let go of the past would be to let go of your value. A true hero is someone who gives of themselves without seeking recognition and looks for opportunities in the present to continue serving others, rather than reliving the glory days of the past.

Each one should use whatever gift he has received to serve others, faithfully administering God's grace in its various forms.
I Peter 4:10 (NIV)

Life That's Predictable

In this case, you live life safe. No risk, no reward. Your past has proven a predictable life, so you repeat it over and over again. You know what you have and you don't dare take the chance of not being in control of your world. You live a boring life, but at least you are the captain of your ship. You do the only thing you know to do, over, and over, and over again. While surrendering control can be frightening, it can open you up to new opportunities and experiences; no one can predict what the day will hold, and you must be willing to walk through the doors God opens when you live in the moment.

Be very careful, then, how you live—not as unwise but as wise, making the most of every opportunity....
Ephesians 5:15-16 (NIV)

LIVING IN THE FUTURE?

The Futurist

You are convinced that if you plan far enough into the future, create a vision board, and just follow the blueprints and manuals, success is a guarantee. You spend time agonizing over pros and cons of decisions that may not even happen, and you are prepared for events long before they take place. The amount of stress you put yourself under to plan for these events prevents you from enjoying day-to-day life. However, manuals and lists cannot prepare you for the curve balls life throws; you must loosen up and live in the present.

Therefore do not worry about tomorrow, for tomorrow will worry about itself. Each day has enough trouble of its own.

Matthew 6:34 (NIV)

The Entrepreneur

You may have more ideas than friends. You spend your life developing ideas instead of relationships (Ouch! … that hurt). Maybe your ideas are successful, and each success is never enough; you also seek further achievement and opportunities. Days turn into months, months into years, and you look back wondering what happened to yesterday. But ultimately, success and ideas aren't fulfilling; you need relationships built on love and trust, not on mutual interest and benefit.

For what will it profit a man if he gains the whole world and forfeits his soul? Or what shall a man give in return for his soul?

Matthew 16:26 (NIV)

The Dreamer

Life is going to get better tomorrow. You are unhappy with today, so you live in a dream world of tomorrow. Your dream world is really an escape from reality, and it is the fix that allows you to function day-to-day. However, if you're always in your head dreaming about the future, you will miss the opportunities in front of you today to create that future. The future God has planned for you may not look like the one you see in your dreams; His future for you is ultimately more beautiful and fulfilling than anything you could ever imagine.

> But as it is written, "Eye has not seen, nor ear heard, nor have entered the heart of man, the things God has prepared for those who love him." *I Corinthians 2:9 (NKJV)*

You may be saying to yourself, *OK, Tammy, I get it, but how do I learn to live in the present? How do I "be still and know that He is God?"* I'm glad you asked. Enjoy your day as a gift from above to have and to hold, and forever love. It's your choice to pick the mind-zone you want to live in. I hope you choose the present. The following coaching exercise will focus your attention on living in the now.

COACHING EXERCISE

1. **Begin to make healthy daily choices.**

   The future is a reflection of your present day-by-day decisions, so make a list of healthy daily habits and check them off throughout the day.

   _____

   _____

   _____

   _____

2. **Look for the reason you are here.**

   You have the ability to make someone's day special. From a smile to holding the door open for someone, your existence matters. See yourself as vital to society. You can extend love to the loveless. Make it your job to improve three people's lives a day. Make a list of ideas below:

   _____

   _____

   _____

   _____

3. **Breathe!**

   As a personal trainer and Pilates instructor, I have learned and experienced the value of deep breathing. This skill will release tension and add serenity to your daily life.

   _____

   _____

   _____

   _____

COACHING EXERCISE

4. Make a thanksgiving list.

Your past may haunt you, and the future may overwhelm you, but what you're thankful for will hold you secure in today.

_____

_____

_____

_____

5. **Just let go.**

We allow so many things to anger, frustrate, and control us. Remember that you have learned the importance of skipping resentment and punishment. A few ways to deal with the pressure of your day are:

a. Walk away from the conflict—stay away long enough for your rational mind to return.

b. Count to twenty then ask yourself if this really matters that much.

c. Breathe and smile.

d. Focus on peace and serenity. Keep inspirational quotes and Scripture near you at all times to reflect upon positive truths.

BECOME A WOMAN OF INFLUENCE

influence (noun): the capacity to have an effect on the character, development, or behavior of someone or something, or the effect itself.

A **Woman of Influence**

uses her lips to speak kindness, her ears to hear pain, her hands to mend brokenness, her heart to give encouragement, and her feet to lead the way.

RECOGNIZE YOUR WORTH

worth (noun): quality that renders something desirable, useful, or valuable; quality that commands esteem or respect.

I praise you because I am fearfully and wonderfully made; your works are wonderful, I know that full well. *Psalm 139:14 (NIV)*

I trust as you have processed through the first two sections of this book that you have made observations as well as taken steps to jump into your future. You have been taking strides down the path to becoming a Woman of Influence, and a Woman of Influence knows who she is and what she has to offer the world; she recognizes her worth.

Many women struggle with self-worth. It is easy in our culture to think there is something wrong with us. We constantly compare ourselves with one another, feeling like we never measure up. We accept poor treatment, stay in harmful relationships, and participate in destructive behavior because deep down, we do not see ourselves as desirable, useful, or valuable. A vital step of becoming a Woman of Influence is learning to love and respect yourself. You must find your value in Christ, the One who created you and knows every part of you, good and bad.

DISCOVER YOUR **VALUE**

I was attending a conference the first time I heard this story. The speaker asked, "Who would like to have a twenty-dollar bill?" Hands went up all over the auditorium. "Great," he said, and then he proceeded to crumple it up a bit. He wadded up the bill and asked, "Now who still wants this twenty-dollar bill?" Once again hands went up all over the room. The speaker then dropped the twenty-dollar bill on the ground and rubbed it into the floor with his shoe. He picked up the crumpled dirty bill. "Now who wants it?" Again hands went up all over the room.

The speaker looked into the crowd and said, "Ladies and gentlemen, you have each learned a valuable lesson today. No matter what I did to the bill, you still want it because its value hasn't changed. Even though it is crumpled and dirty, it's still worth twenty dollars. Although someone may have been misused and abused, he or she still has the same infinite worth. Every person is precious in God's sight."

This story came to mind when I first met Toni at a girls' study at a university in my community. Toni was somewhat reluctant to come with her friends—she was afraid that once I got to know more about her, I would judge her. Her friends reassured her that she was safe with me, and Toni began showing up to the group.

The first time Toni came, she sat as far back as possible, ready to make a mad dash if necessary. The next time she came, she sat closer with the girls and even participated a bit in the conversation. I did not know Toni's story, but I could tell right away that she had a wall of protection all around her. Week by week, she showed up to hear my coaching sessions on worth and integrity.

One Tuesday night after our study, Toni approached me with a question. Asking to meet with me privately was a big step for her, but God was touching her heart. As we sat and had coffee, Toni began to share her story with me: "I'm afraid if I tell you more about myself and what my job is, you might not like me."

"That's impossible! I already like you, and what you do for a living will never change whether I like you or not," I assured her. Then I asked, "What is it, Toni? What are you afraid to tell me?"

Toni began to share about her childhood and how life had changed for her in high school. As a child she grew up in what appeared to be a happy home. Her parents both worked full time on opposite shifts. Her father worked mornings so that Toni's mother could be home with her during the day, then her mother worked an evening shift so her father could be with her at night. It seemed to all work great in Toni's little eyes—it was her normal view of family life.

As Toni grew older she started to notice her mother and father did not do many things together. They did not go on family vacations, attend church, or share meals at the same time. But Toni thought that her family was just different from her friends.

Then one day in high school as Toni was getting ready to leave, she heard her parents arguing about what was best for her. "She is better off with me," her father said. "No, she is not. I am her mother, and we are very close. It is only right for her to live with me."

At first Toni could not believe her ears. *What are they talking about? Are they getting a divorce? Is this about me?* Toni's thoughts were racing in her mind as she stormed out the door. Life changed in an instant that day, and Toni's world would never look the same.

When her parents separated, Toni saw the divorce as betrayal, and she moved out of the house at seventeen, determined to make it on her own. Withdrawing from them both, she thought she would get even by becoming successful and showing her parents she did not need them.

Her desire to make it on her own was such a strong driving force that it didn't matter how she achieved her goal. Once she got to college, she started looking for a job. A new friend in her dorm told her that the local bar was hiring dancers and that she could make a lot of money really fast.

Initially, Toni thought she could never do that. But then little by little she thought about how she really needed the money and this might be a good way to get ahead. Toni's heart had grown numb, and she reasoned that she would only be doing this to get through college. Once she graduated she would be able to get a really great job and move past this nightmare.

What she did not expect was to be challenged by her own conscience. As she listened week after week to the coaching sessions on worth and value, her heart began to soften.

"So that's it…I make money using my body," she finished. "That's what I do. That is how I get through college. That is how I pay my bills. Now you know. See, it's bad… I told you that you would not like me."

I looked right into her eyes and said, "First of all, I still like you very much…but the real issue here is, it doesn't matter how much I like you; it only matters how much you like yourself."

She paused and looked up at me and said, "What does that even mean?"

"It means I am not the one who matters. Your worth and dignity is something that comes from God and dwells deep inside you, and once you understand that, you will only do and say the things that bring you value."

Our coffee time together lasted much longer than I had planned, yet the time flew by as my heart became tethered to hers. I was moved with both compassion and sorrow—compassion for all she had been through, and sorrow for how she felt judged by the world. I agreed to meet with Toni on a weekly basis to help her understand her worth and integrity.

We worked on fundamental concepts of value, starting with the fact that we are created in God's image (Genesis 1:27), and that God creates who we are on the inside and the outside (Psalm 139:13-17, see below). God does not create mistakes. He knows all of our weaknesses and strengths, just like a potter knows every imperfection and curve in his bowls and vases.

In time, Toni changed jobs, making more money as a waitress than she did in the club. But the best part was she came to discover her value through God's eyes. She memorized and meditated upon Scripture that was uplifting and edifying, and she is now embracing the love of her Heavenly Father.

BELIEVE GOD'S OPINION

Most women who struggle with self-worth just haven't taken the time to get to know who they truly are or how God sees them. Many of us allow others' opinions to shape our self-worth; we do not feel secure unless someone else is telling us we are beautiful, smart, funny, or competent. If we lose that reinforcement from those around us, we will seek it wherever and however we can find it: an insecure person goes on shopping sprees, begins affairs, becomes a workaholic, accepts abuse, and so on. However, a Woman of Influence recognizes that her value doesn't come from any single person; her worth is foremost in God's eyes, and His opinion is the only one that truly counts. She has been bought with the price of Christ. She recites truths like:

- I am worth more than money.
- I am worth more than abuse.
- I am worth more than laziness.
- I am worth more than fear.
- I am worth more than excuses.
- I am worth more than past mistakes.
- I am worth the love of a Savior.

In her book *God Loves Ugly*, my friend Christa Black Gifford shares her battles with self-hatred and insecurity. She fought eating disorders, depression, and addiction in her search for self-worth, and understanding her worth in God's sight was not a belief that came easily.

A Woman of Influence recognizes that **her value** doesn't come from any single person; **her worth** is foremost in God's eyes, and His opinion is the only one that **truly counts.**

Like too many young girls today, Christa experienced sexual abuse as a child. Those memories translated into feelings of unworthiness and shame that she could not explain. A mentality of brokenness led to more unhealthy thoughts and behaviors, which in turn left Christa lost and alone. Looking in the mirror only reminded her how of how ugly she felt each day. Christa looked for happiness in all the wrong places and through all the wrong people.

Over her senior spring break in high school, Christa's parents made her attend a church service. She sat unmoved and defiant through the worship service, but then something unexpected began to happen that changed her life forever. A woman began playing the violin, an instrument that Christa had been playing since she was three years old. Somehow the melody of that song began to soften her rebellious heart. That night, Christa released her resentment and anger, and received the overpowering love of an almighty God who knows her better than she knows herself.

Christa chose to accept the peace of God and the unconditional love He gives. She opened her heart to His opinion of her as His beautiful daughter, and He took away the guilt and shame that she carried.

I have seen firsthand the impact Christa's story has had on countless women. She has been able to reach out to broken women and not only speak to them, but also write beautiful songs of love and encouragement.

In Psalm 139, David speaks of our worth and value to God, describing how intimately God knows us. Read this beautiful psalm that portrays the depth to which God loves each one of us:

You have searched me, Lord, and you know me. You know when I sit and when I rise; you perceive my thoughts from afar. You discern my going out and my lying down; you are familiar with all my ways. Before a word is on my tongue you, Lord, know it completely. You hem me in behind and before, and you lay your hand upon me. Such knowledge is too wonderful for me, too lofty for me to attain. Where can I go from your Spirit? Where can I flee from your presence? If I go up to the heavens, you are there; if I make my bed in the depths, you are there. If I rise on the wings of the dawn, if I settle on the far side of the sea, even there your hand will guide me, your right hand will hold me fast. If I say, "Surely the darkness will hide me and the light become night around me," even the darkness will not be dark to you; the night will shine like the day, for darkness is as light to you. For you created my inmost being; you knit me together in my mother's womb. I praise you because I am fearfully and wonderfully made; your works are wonderful, I know that full well. My frame was not hidden from you when I was made in the secret place, when I was woven together in the depths of the earth. Your eyes saw my unformed body; all the days ordained for me were written in your book before one of them came to be. How precious to me are your thoughts, God! How vast is the sum of them! Were I to count them, they would outnumber the grains of sand—when I awake, I am still with you. ...Search me, God, and know my heart; test me and know my anxious thoughts. See if there is any offensive way in me, and lead me in the way everlasting.
(Psalm 139:1-18, 23-24, NIV)

KEYS TO FINDING YOUR WORTH

The struggle for self-worth is an ongoing battle for many of us. However, the following steps will direct your focus when you feel unworthy and insecure.

Believe the God of the Universe Loves You

I often hear people say "God is too busy for my little stuff; I'll just save the BIG stuff for Him." The problem with this philosophy is God doesn't have a scale for stuff. He moves the Universe the same way he moves a pen... Effortlessly. This is the same way He approaches loving you. There is nothing you must do to receive His love or anything you can do to lose His love. It's endless and forever. All you need to do is accept the fact that the God who created the universe is the same God who created you, and He loves His handiwork. Until you embrace His "Open Arms" policy, you will never truly understand the love of the Father.

Believe You Have Something to Offer

I love watching people's lives change as they begin to understand their worth in this world. For some reason most of us have to be encouraged, coached, or convinced that we have something to offer others. We minimize our importance, worth, and purpose in this life, but the truth is that what you have to offer others is YOU. I love the simple messages from God. We come into this world with nothing and we leave the same way. It is not what we acquire that makes a difference in the lives of others. It's what we give away that changes the world. That gift is you.

Stop Looking Elsewhere

Our human nature tries to validate our worth through achievements and relationships. We search for approval and admiration by getting job promotions, earning credentials, or making social connections. While these pursuits are not necessarily wrong, they do not elevate your worth one degree. The Bible tells us our worth is found through Christ alone. God values your life so much that He gave His son for you. You are a child of the King of Kings; therefore, you are crowned with royalty. The seed of worth was planted in you at birth. Water it with faith and confidence and see it grow into a life full of purpose and meaning.

Stay Focused on the Truth

You can know something in your mind, yet your emotions can throw you under the bus. I may agree with someone that I have worth and purpose, and then in a matter of moments have feelings of low self-esteem and insecurity. The only way to battle negative feelings is to stay focused on the truth. Write out Bible verses that remind you of your worth and put them in prominent places—on the bathroom or bedroom mirror, next to the computer, on the dashboard of your car.

LIFE MAP ASSESSMENT

As a Life Coach, I have seen many things that have the potential to cripple our vision, passion, and ability, and that prevent us from moving forward into becoming Women of Influence. With almost all of my clients I use the Life Map Assessment to start them on the journey of self-discovery. I am introducing it in this chapter because I see it as a powerful tool for you to begin understanding your worth and value, and it will be a meaningful tool for examining your identity and destiny as you move forward as well.

What is a Life Map?

The goal of a Life Map is to meet and love yourself. A Life Map provides a visual model of your life experience. Each of us is unique. We all experience life in a different way, and that is what makes us who we are today and who we are on the way to becoming. The Life Map allows you to take those experiences and, for the first time, put them in a form where you can see yourself at a glance.

A Life Map will enable you to understand your unique operating style. Do you ever wonder what drives your decision-making process or why you respond to things differently than a friend or family member might? Your Life Map will provide insight into your unique drivers and how to use these to achieve your goals. You can stop questioning, "Why do I do that?" in a negative way, and instead gain empowerment to use your unique operating style to move yourself forward.

A Life Map will assist you in the discovery of your encoded thread of passion—what you really love to do! Your unique experience and your unique operating style come together in this visual model to empower you to use your unique passions to live the life you truly want to live.

The First Stage

Before we begin the mapping process, we're going to start by going down memory lane. Focus on remembering as much as possible of the different stages of your life. The highlights of this information will go into your Life Map.

The following pages contain sets of questions. Try to answer as many as relate to you. These are prompts to help you tell your story in your own way. Don't worry about grammar or spelling, just put down whatever you can remember. For some of the questions relating to your earlier years, you may need to talk to someone who knew you then, like a parent or other close relative. Remember, there are no wrong answers to these questions—there are only *your* answers.

At times this assessment may be difficult. We all have positive and negative memories, and all of those contribute to who we are. Be okay with going back into difficult times. These are as much a part of us as the good times.

Also, take your time. The more you put into this exercise, the more you will get out of it in the end. Put thought and detail into your responses and try to think about why you felt or acted the way you did at the time the events happened. This is who you are. This is how you uncover the things that are unique about you and make you stand out from everyone else.

"There is no greater agony than
bearing an *untold story*
inside you." ~ Maya Angelou

Where did you grow up?

_____

_____

_____

_____

_____

_____

Describe your home. What was your favorite part of the home?
What part did you like the least?

_____

_____

_____

_____

_____

_____

Did you have pets? If so, what kind?

_____

_____

_____

_____

_____

_____

"Find out who you are and do it on purpose."
Dolly Parton

What was your favorite thing to do as a small child?

_____

_____

_____

_____

_____

Were you shy as a child or were you outgoing?

_____

_____

_____

_____

_____

_____

What is the best thing you remember about your childhood?

_____

_____

_____

_____

_____

_____

"One that would have the fruit must climb the tree."

Thomas Fuller

Were there any painful times in your childhood?

_____

_____

_____

_____

_____

_____

Who did you look up to as a child?

_____

_____

_____

_____

_____

_____

What was your first day of school like?

_____

_____

_____

_____

_____

_____

"You must do the thing you think you cannot do."

Eleanor Roosevelt

Describe your best friend in elementary school.

_____

_____

_____

_____

_____

_____

What was your favorite thing about elementary school?

_____

_____

_____

_____

_____

_____

What did you like the least about elementary school?

_____

_____

_____

_____

_____

_____

"Cast all your anxiety on Him because He cares for you."
1 Peter 5:7 (NIV)

Describe your bedroom. How did you decorate it?

_____

_____

_____

_____

_____

_____

What were your favorite activities growing up?

_____

_____

_____

_____

_____

Who did you look up to as you grow older?

_____

_____

_____

_____

_____

_____

"You must have control of the authorship of your own destiny.
The pen that writes your life story must be held in your own hand."
Irene C. Kassorla

Did you live in one place growing up or did you move around?

_____

_____

_____

_____

_____

_____

Did you have any hobbies as a child?

_____

_____

_____

_____

_____

Were there any other significant things about your childhood that stand out to you?

_____

_____

_____

_____

_____

_____

"Learn to...be what you are and learn to resign with a good grace
all that you are not."
Henri Frederic Amiel

Describe your junior high or high school experience.

_____

_____

_____

_____

_____

_____

What were your favorite things about junior high/high school?

_____

_____

_____

_____

_____

What were your least favorite things about junior high/high school?

_____

_____

_____

_____

_____

_____

"He who trims himself to suit everyone will soon whittle himself away."

Raymond Hull

What activities were you involved in?

_____

_____

_____

_____

_____

What were your favorite subjects?

_____

_____

_____

_____

_____

What were your least favorite subjects?

_____

_____

_____

_____

_____

_____

"You were born an original. Don't die a copy."

John Mason

Who was your best friend in your teens?

_____

_____

_____

_____

_____

_____

What were your hobbies as a teen?

_____

_____

_____

_____

_____

Who did you look up to as a teen?

_____

_____

_____

_____

_____

_____

_____

"Sometimes when I consider what tremendous consequences come from little things, I am tempted to think there are no little things."

Bruce Barton

How did you relate to your family as a teen?

_____

_____

_____

_____

_____

_____

Are there any other significant things about your teenage years that stand out to you?

_____

_____

_____

_____

Did you go to college? If so, where?

_____

_____

_____

_____

_____

_____

"Forgiveness means letting go of a hurtful situation and moving on with your own happiness."

Amanda Ford

What subject did you major in?

_____

_____

_____

_____

_____

Did you join a fraternity or sorority?

_____

_____

_____

_____

_____

If you didn't go to college, what did you do after high school?

_____

_____

_____

_____

_____

_____

"Be willing to be a beginner every single morning."

Meister Eckhart

Did you stay close to home after high school or did you move a distance away?

_____

_____

_____

_____

_____

_____

What attracted you to the path you chose after high school?

_____

_____

_____

_____

_____

_____

Who did you look up to at this time of your life?

_____

_____

_____

_____

_____

_____

_____

"When one door closes, another opens; but we often look so long and so regretfully upon the closed door that we do not see the one which has opened for us."

Alexander Graham Bell

Who was your best friend at this time?

_____

_____

_____

_____

_____

_____

What are your favorite memories of this time?

_____

_____

_____

_____

_____

What are your least favorite memories of this time?

_____

_____

_____

_____

_____

*"The wise man must remember that while he is a descendant of the past,
he is a parent of the future."*

Herbert Spencer

What have you done since college?

_____

_____

_____

_____

_____

_____

What do you like the most about what you do now?

_____

_____

_____

_____

_____

What do you like the least about what you do now?

_____

_____

_____

_____

_____

"Changes are not only possible and predictable, but to deny them is to be an accomplice to one's own necessary vegetation."

Gail Sheehy

If you could do anything and get paid for it, what would it be?

_____

_____

_____

_____

_____

_____

Who are the significant people in your life now?

_____

_____

_____

_____

_____

Who are you closest to in your family?

_____

_____

_____

_____

_____

"Here is the test to find whether your mission on Earth is finished:
If you're alive, it isn't."
Richard Bach

What is your favorite thing about your home?

_____

_____

_____

_____

_____

_____

_____

What significant things have happened to you over the years since high school that have made an impact on you?

_____

_____

_____

_____

_____

_____

_____

"Peace I leave with you; My peace I give you. I do not give to you as the world gives. Do not let your hearts be troubled and do not be afraid."

John 14:27 (NIV)

Add any additional thoughts or expand on any of the items above that stand out to you.

_____

_____

_____

_____

_____

_____

_____

_____

_____

_____

_____

_____

_____

_____

_____

_____

_____

_____

_____

_____

_____

HOW TO CREATE A LIFE MAP

Now that you've had a chance to put your memories on paper, we'll give you the steps for creating your own Life Map.

STEP 1

DIVIDE YOUR LIFE INTO FOUR STAGES:

Early Years

These are your early childhood years through kindergarten. During this time your family is usually the strongest influence in your life.

Preparation Years

These are the years you spent in elementary school. Family is still a strong influence, but you begin to make your own friends and develop your own personality.

Formation Years

These are your junior high/high school years, the time where you develop your individuality.

Clarification Years

These are the years after high school, where your life experiences coalesce and you choose a career and start your own family.

STEP 2

CREATE AN OUTLINE FOR EACH STAGE:

Answer the following five questions for each life stage:

What were the high points?
What were the happy times, the times that you look back on fondly?
These are the times that you would relive if you could.

EARLY YEARS:

_____

_____

_____

_____

_____

_____

_____

_____

PREPARATION YEARS:

_____

_____

_____

_____

_____

_____

_____

_____

FORMATION YEARS:

_____

_____

_____

_____

_____

_____

_____

_____

_____

_____

CLARIFICATION YEARS:

_____

_____

_____

_____

_____

_____

_____

_____

_____

_____

_____

What were the low points?
These are the painful times. This could be a time of personal pain or a time when family or friends faced adversity.

EARLY YEARS:

_____

_____

_____

_____

_____

_____

_____

_____

PREPARATION YEARS:

_____

_____

_____

_____

_____

_____

_____

_____

_____

FORMATION YEARS:

_____

_____

_____

_____

_____

_____

_____

_____

_____

_____

CLARIFICATION YEARS:

_____

_____

_____

_____

_____

_____

_____

_____

_____

_____

_____

_____

What were the bridges or tunnels that enabled you to cross a barrier?

What enabled you to get through a difficult time? This can be a place, an activity, or an attitude that you used to enable you to deal with adversity. It may be healthy and positive or unhealthy and negative.

EARLY YEARS:

_____

_____

_____

_____

_____

_____

_____

_____

PREPARATION YEARS:

_____

_____

_____

_____

_____

_____

_____

_____

FORMATION YEARS:

_____

_____

_____

_____

_____

_____

_____

_____

_____

_____

_____

CLARIFICATION YEARS:

_____

_____

_____

_____

_____

_____

_____

_____

_____

_____

_____

_____

What were the centers of energy?
These are places or activities that recharge you or focus you and drive you forward. Many people find energy in solitude. Others may find energy interacting with others.

EARLY YEARS:

_____

_____

_____

_____

_____

_____

_____

_____

_____

_____

PREPARATION YEARS:

_____

_____

_____

_____

_____

_____

_____

_____

_____

_____

FORMATION YEARS:

_____

_____

_____

_____

_____

_____

_____

_____

_____

_____

CLARIFICATION YEARS:

_____

_____

_____

_____

_____

_____

_____

_____

_____

_____

_____

Who were your heroes?

Who were the people you looked up to? They may be people in your life, people in the news, historical figures, or even fictional characters. Typically, we are attracted to people who are like us. By examining the people that we look up to we can learn more about ourselves.

EARLY YEARS:

_____

_____

_____

_____

_____

_____

_____

_____

_____

PREPARATION YEARS:

_____

_____

_____

_____

_____

_____

_____

_____

_____

FORMATION YEARS:

_____

_____

_____

_____

_____

_____

_____

_____

_____

_____

_____

CLARIFICATION YEARS:

_____

_____

_____

_____

_____

_____

_____

_____

_____

_____

_____

STEP 3

RATE YOUR EXPERIENCES

Rate the positive or negative impact of each experience on a scale of −10 to +10. A +10 rating would be for the happiest and most energizing experiences. A −10 rating would be for the most painful experiences. Place your ratings in the margin next to each entry.

STEP 4

PLOT THE POINTS

Now transfer the information from your answers onto the Life Map. You can use the Map in the following pages, use your own paper to create a large Map, or download one at www.WomenofInfluence.today. Some people plot the points of events across the years and connect them with a line. Others plot sections of their lives in a general range (+10 for the early years, for example) and then plot any points that relate to specific items that run through those ranges.

STEP 5

IDENTIFY KEY WORDS

Look for key words that describe the dominant themes in your Life Map. For example, three key words from the events in my Life Map are faith, fashion, and fitness. Add these in the space provided on the Map. When we're done with the Life Map, you're going to be able to see your life based on a few words, and I'm going to ask you to articulate or define or explain yourself in three to four words.

USE THIS ADDITIONAL SPACE FOR ANY NOTES OR THOUGHTS YOU HAVE DURING THIS EXERCISE.

LIFE MAP

	EARLY YEARS	PREPARATION YEARS

+10

+5

-5

-10

FORMATION YEARS   CLARIFICATION YEARS

www.womanofInfluence.today

ANALYZING YOUR LIFE MAP

STEP 1

PEAKS & VALLEYS

Note the dominant highs and lows throughout each of the four stages of your life. Compare the peaks then the valleys to answer the following questions:

EARLY YEARS:

What do the peaks have in common? The valleys?

_____

_____

_____

_____

_____

How did you feel during those times?

_____

_____

_____

_____

What effect do they have on you today?

_____

_____

_____

_____

"How many cares one loses when one decides not to be something but to be someone." Gabrielle "Coco" Chanel

PREPARATION YEARS:

What do the peaks have in common? The valleys?

_____

_____

_____

_____

_____

How did you feel during those times?

_____

_____

_____

_____

_____

What effect do they have on you today?

_____

_____

_____

_____

_____

"Life is no brief candle to me. It is a sort of splendid torch which I have got hold of for the moment, and I want to make it burn as brightly as possible before handing it on to future generations."

George Bernard Shaw

FORMATION YEARS:

What do the peaks have in common? The valleys?

_____

_____

_____

_____

_____

_____

How did you feel during those times?

_____

_____

_____

_____

_____

_____

What effect do they have on you today?

_____

_____

_____

_____

_____

_____

_____

"One day your life will flash before your eyes. Make sure it's worth watching."
Gerard Way

CLARIFICATION YEARS:

What do the peaks have in common? The valleys?

_____

_____

_____

_____

_____

_____

How did you feel during those times?

_____

_____

_____

_____

_____

_____

What effect do they have on you today?

_____

_____

_____

_____

_____

_____

"So many of our dreams at first seems impossible, then they seem improbable, and then, when we summon the will, they soon become inevitable."
Christopher Reeve

STEP 2

USING YOUR LIFE MAP, ANSWER THE FOLLOWING QUESTIONS.

When I think of the person who has made the strongest positive impact on my life, I believe he or she has had a powerful influence on me because:

_____

_____

_____

_____

_____

The qualities of character I most admire in others are:

_____

_____

_____

_____

_____

I am impressed by the following attitudes:

_____

_____

_____

_____

The three people whom I feel have accomplished the most with their lives are:

_____

_____

_____

_____

How have they accomplished this?

_____

_____

_____

_____

_____

The three people whom I know that are the happiest are _____
because _____.

_____

_____

_____

_____

If I had unlimited resources I would:

_____

_____

_____

_____

The moments of greatest happiness and satisfaction come to me when:

_____

_____

_____

_____

_____

The people who know me well tell me that my greatest strength is:

_____

_____

_____

_____

_____

The one thing that brings me the greatest satisfaction is:

_____

_____

_____

_____

_____

The three most admirable qualities of my life are:

_____

_____

_____

_____

_____

My top three priorities in life are:

_____

_____

_____

_____

_____

The thing about my personal life I am most proud of is:

_____

_____

_____

_____

_____

_____

STEP 3

REHEARSE YOUR LIFE MAP

Share your Life Map with at least one other person—invite them to ask questions. We learn a lot through journaling and reviewing our own memories. However, we can learn even more when we tell our story to someone else. There may be things that we could dig deeper into. The probing questions of someone else can cause us to reevaluate things that we may have passed over when we worked through our journaling process. Additionally, someone who knew us when we were younger may have insight into our earlier lives that we may not remember.

"Your imagination is your preview of life's coming attractions."

Albert Einstein

Do you feel you know yourself better now? The Life Map Assessment is a way to learn who you really are and to understand that God has called you into being exactly who you are. Understanding your unique story and how it shapes who you are today is a key to setting your goals for the future. Only you can do the things that you will achieve—God has a purpose and a plan for you. Embrace this knowledge and embrace yourself! You are now empowered to move forward.

CHAPTER EIGHT

EMBRACE YOUR IDENTITY

identity (noun): the distinguishing character or personality of an individual.

Charm is deceptive and beauty is fleeting, but a woman who fears the Lord is to be praised. *Proverbs 31:30 (NIV)*

I don't believe there is an area women struggle with more than with their identity. Many women search for their identity through careers, children, success, money, or ministry. We long to be known and appreciated, so we associate our identity with something or someone. However, often who we show ourselves to be on the outside doesn't match who we are or who we want to be on the inside. Sometimes we feel like we have to wear different masks for different people, and we forget who we were to begin with.

True identity is a balance of our physical identity, which is a product of our experiences and personalities, and our spiritual identity, which comes from our relationship with Christ. Both have to be balanced to have a healthy life. Understanding and embracing all aspects of your identity—your experiences, personality, and relationship with God—is key to becoming a Woman of Influence.

OUR EXPERIENCES

This chapter has been very insightful for me to write. It has both confirmed and further defined my thoughts on identity. I have been known as an employee, Life Coach, friend, neighbor, daughter, mother, and wife. I'll never forget a warm summer day when my kids were young, and I was faced with asking myself the question, *Who am I, and what happened to my life?*

I had just dropped my son Jeremy off at football practice, then raced off to take Josh to drama rehearsal, before dropping off Jennie at her dance lesson. I had started my family very quickly after marriage, and my three beautiful children had become my life. Like many women today, I loved being a stay-at-home mom. My kids were the joy of my life and that kept me very busy. But for just a moment I thought to myself, *Where did my life go?*

As I sat in the car waiting to start the pick-up rounds, I reminisced about my youth and all the plans I had for my life. I had hoped to travel and teach, go on missions and host charity events, and possibly one day write a book. In my mind and dreams, I saw myself doing it all.

Shortly after taking a stroll down memory lane, I realized it was time to start gathering the troops. First Jeremy came running to the car. "Mom, you won't believe it. I caught a pass then ran eighty yards for a touchdown! Mom, it was amazing—I am so excited. I love football, and I love you, too!" He chatted the whole time I was driving to the next pick-up destination.

No sooner had he taken a breath than Josh jumped in the car. "Guess what guys? I got the lead role in the drama. I can't believe it! Mom, they really liked me. You said I could do it. You were right." As the boys shared success stories from their day, I beamed with pure joy. There is nothing like having your children feel good about themselves and accepted by others. As I pulled up to pick up the last of the clan, my little Jennie came running out, tutu in hand. "Mommy, can Ashley eat dinner with us and spend the night? Please mommy, please?" Off we went three kids plus one with my heart singing. For that moment I was living out what some would call my identity— Mom—at least for a season of life.

Now my children are grown and have children of their own. Most days, my identity as Mom is in the background. When the nest finally empties, many women who have only defined themselves as mothers find themselves questioning their identities. Likewise, in a society that places so much emphasis on careers, many people find their identities wrapped up in their careers. We begin asking tiny children what they want to be when they grow up, and the question follows them through the rest of their lives. It's no wonder we see our jobs as a reflection of who we are and attach our identities to them.

When I met Arlene, she was an executive with a high-profile oil company. She started working for the company at a young age and quickly moved up the ranks to Senior Vice President within a matter of years. Her life was wed deeply in the company and her dream of financial success had become a reality. Arlene worked long hours and had little time for a social life. It never really bothered her because she was living her dream. At work, she was "one of the boys," and she loved being in the club.

Over time, the pressure of big decisions and daily competition began taking a toll and her joy began to diminish. The once-young executives were beginning to rise in position and expertise. Arlene found herself staying up late at night just to keep up with them in knowledge. Angst and anxiety had become her two new companions, and she slowly starting dreading her job. The board of directors decided that Jonas, a new upcoming director, would shadow Arlene for the next few months. Arlene knew what this meant. She was slowly being replaced with younger minds and quicker results.

Arlene was having an **identity crisis.** She had become one with her position and had mistaken her career with her personal identity.

Sitting across the table from me at our first coaching session, she asked me, "What am I going to do? This is all I know. This is who I am. My whole identity is in this job, and I would be lost without it!" The words came out of her mouth, "What have I done? What have I become?"

Arlene was having an identity crisis. She had become one with her position and had mistaken her career with her personal identity. I could see the expression on her face quickly change. All at once Arlene realized she had allowed her high profile position to define her. She had forfeited the best years of her life for a company that only saw her as a commodity.

No matter what we spend our time doing, whether we're paid or not, we see our identity as what we do or what we give. While some deal with Johnny climbing up their legs, others are climbing the corporate ladder, and those duties become their identities. However, our identity is more than just our experiences. If I have lost my identity as a mother, do I cease to have identity? Of course not! What if I change careers, lose my mother, move away from friends and family, and start life all over—do I lose my identity? Again the answer is simply *No!* What I do is only *part* of my identity. Remember, our identities are a combination of our experiences, personality, and relationship with God, so if our lives change, our identities are not lost. We may need time to readjust to the changes, but we are all individuals with unique dreams, goals, and gifts, and God still has a plan for each of us.

OUR PERSONALITIES

I grew up in a home with three sisters. We all have the same parents, went to the same schools with mostly the same teachers, ate the same meals at dinner, went to the same church on Sundays, had the same pet, sometimes even wore the same clothes, yet we are as different as pie and peas. When we get together for family events, it's almost comical how different we each respond to various topics. It doesn't matter if we discuss children, faith, even the weather—we all have personal opinions. In spite of the fact that we are all blood-related and have shared many of the same experiences, we each have radically different personalities that contribute greatly to our different identities.

I have created an assessment that will help you begin to understand and embrace who you truly are, as well as how to understand the traits, behaviors, and reactions of family members, friends, and colleagues. You were born with certain characteristics and a personality that will be a part of your life forever. We can learn to develop or control these traits, but for the most part, they will define our behavior forever.

WHAT SHAPE ARE YOU?

This assessment is based on Hippocrates' theory of human moods. He identified four basic behaviors that are dominant in individuals. Everyone has a basic personality type, and by identifying yours, you will better understand yourself and can learn how to relate, communicate, and respond to the other basic personalities.

I have taken the four basic personality temperaments and associated them with different shapes. I believe these shapes represent the characteristic of each personality.

- Opinionated Square
- Outgoing Circle
- Organized Triangle
- Observant Octagon

STRENGTHS

In the following table, review each set of four key words then circle the one that is most like you in the Strengths table. You may find that more than one word in a set applies to you; however, choose the one that has the greatest application to your personality.

Ambitious: Goal-oriented, driven visionary
Animated: Expressive, engaging player
Accommodating: Helpful, considerate peacemaker
Artistic: Creative, talented designer

Cordial: Polite, considerate team player
Capable: Competent, effective project leader
Cultivated: Thoughtful, informed scholar
Charming: Entertaining, appealing storyteller

Disciplined: Structured, detailed problem-solver
Dependable: Steady, reliable friend
Dynamic: Active, charismatic engager
Determined: Focused, dedicated achiever

Empowered: Confident, bold individual
Energetic: Enthusiastic, vivacious go-getter

Exact: Meticulous, economical thinker
Even-keeled: Calm, stable anchor

Fearless: Bold: aggressive decision-maker
Faithful: Loyal defender
Funny: Comical, silly entertainer
Flexible: Easy-going, adaptive player

Inspirational: Influential, enlivening motivator
Inoffensive: Pleasant, neutral diplomat
Intuitive: Perceptive observer
Independent: Self-sufficient individual

Listener: Sympathetic, kind counselor
Likeable: Affable, friendly charmer
List-maker: Thorough, prepared planner
Leader: Assertive authoritative figure

Outgoing: Gregarious, colorful personality
Organized: Ordered, tidy arranger
Observant: Attentive people-watcher
Opinionated: Assertive, decisive spokesperson

Persistent: Tenacious competitor
Positive: Upbeat optimist
Patient: Tolerant, understanding forgiver
Perfectionist: Person with high standards

Trustworthy: Reliable person of integrity
Talkative: Friendly communicator
Tough: Brave, resilient contender
Tactful: Careful, discrete commenter

1	Ambitious	Animated	Accommodating	Artistic
2	Cordial	Capable	Cultivated	Charming
3	Disciplined	Dependable	Dynamic	Determined
4	Empowered	Energetic	Exact	Even-keeled
5	Fearless	Faithful	Funny	Flexible
6	Inspirational	Inoffensive	Intuitive	Independent
7	Listener	Likeable	List-maker	Leader
8	Outgoing	Organized	Observant	Opinionated
9	Persistent	Positive	Patient	Perfectionist
10	Trustworthy	Talkative	Tough	Tactful

WEAKNESSES

Now follow the same process with these key word groupings that apply to your weaknesses. Be honest! None of us likes to admit where we go wrong. Assessing yourself accurately is important to understanding your personality profile and how you can make improvements.

Arrogant: Boasts in success
Antisocial: Avoids people and parties
Agitated: Becomes annoyed quickly
Aloof: Remains distant and removed

Doubtful: Questions others' motivations
Distant: Remains removed from the group
Discontent: Needs affirmation
Detached: Treats plans with indifference

Fearful: Resists new ideas or settings
Fixated: Obsesses on goal or project
Fickle: Shifts moods and opinions
Flighty: Gets distracted or forgetful

Impatient: Lacks tolerance or self-control
Impulsive: Acts without thinking
Indecisive: Fails to make choices
Insecure: Belittles self and seeks approval

Irritable: Gets upset by others' mistakes
Isolated: Prefers to be alone
Inattentive: Overlooks details and doesn't listen
Indifferent: Lacks interest or enthusiasm

Nitpicking: Fixates on details and imperfections
Nervous: Worries frequently
Noisy: Talks and tells stories for attention
Know-It-All: Thinks their ideas are superior

Shy: Withdraws from involvement
Sloppy: Lacks organization
Scheming: Plots ways to get ahead
Spiteful: Antagonizes others

Unemotional: Avoids expressing feelings
Unmotivated: Lacks drive and discipline
Unpredictable: Acts on desire or emotion
Unhappy: Fails to see positives

Querulous: Finds fault and is difficult to please
Quick-tempered: Reacts negatively to criticism
Quarrelsome: Responds defensively
Quiet: Keeps thoughts to themselves

Careless: Forgets details or responsibilities
Cautious: Resists being forced into decisions
Cynical: Undercuts positivity
Contrary: Argues for the sake of argument

1	Arrogant	Antisocial	Agitated	Aloof
2	Doubtful	Distant	Discontent	Detached
3	Fearful	Fixated	Fickle	Flighty
4	Impatient	Impulsive	Indecisive	Insecure
5	Irritable	Isolated	Inattentive	Indifferent
6	Nitpicking	Nervous	Noisy	Know-It-All
7	Shy	Sloppy	Scheming	Spiteful
8	Unemotional	Unmotivated	Unpredictable	Unhappy
9	Querulous	Quick-tempered	Quarrelsome	Quiet
10	Cautious	Careless	Cynical	Contrary

Locate your circled key words from the previous tables and circle them in the table below. Total the number of circled words in each column at the bottom of the Strengths and Weaknesses tables and add the two totals together. Whichever column has the most circled words will reveal your personality shape!

STRENGTHS

	Circle	**Square**	**Triangle**	**Octagon**
1	Animated	Ambitious	Artistic	Accommodating
2	Charming	Capable	Cultivated	Cordial
3	Dynamic	Determined	Disciplined	Dependable
4	Energetic	Empowered	Exact	Even-Keeled
5	Funny	Fearless	Faithful	Flexible
6	Inspirational	Independent	Intuitive	Inoffensive
7	Likeable	Leader	List-Maker	Listener
8	Outgoing	Opinionated	Organized	Observant
9	Positive	Persistent	Perfectionist	Patient
10	Talkative	Tough	Trustworthy	Tactful

WEAKNESSES

	Circle	Square	Triangle	Octagon
1	Agitated	Arrogant	Antisocial	Aloof
2	Discontent	Distant	Doubtful	Detached
3	Flighty	Fixated	Fickle	Fearful
4	Impulsive	Impatient	Insecure	Indecisive
5	Inattentive	Irritable	Isolated	Indifferent
6	Noisy	Know-It-All	Nitpicking	Nervous
7	Sloppy	Scheming	Spiteful	Shy
8	Unpredictable	Unemotional	Unhappy	Unmotivated
9	Quick-tempered	Quarrelsome	Querulous	Quiet
10	Careless	Contrary	Cynical	Cautious

Below is a synopsis of each of the personality shapes. Find your shape below to see a snapshot of your personality highlights, as well as pointers on how to best communicate with other personalities who fit into this shape. Use this information to learn more about yourself and about your family, friends, and peers.

OUTGOING CIRCLE

Strengths	Outgoing, Friendly, Communicative, Energetic
Weaknesses	Rushes, Restless, Disorganized, Emotional
Desires	Activity, Sincerity, Being Heard, Enthusiasm
Avoids	Alone Time, Keeping a Schedule, Follow-Through, Details
Ability	Encouragement, Inspiration, Raising Support

When relating with a **CIRCLE:**

- Be warm and relational.
- Keep the conversation light and positive.
- Ask about their ideas and opinions.

Areas of contention and frustration:

- Asking for details and facts.
- Trying to control the conversation.
- Appearing to be in a hurry and uninterested.

OPINIONATED SQUARE

Strengths	Bold, Competitive, Adventurous, Leader
Weaknesses	Overbearing, Argumentative, Driven, Demanding
Desires	Respect, Recognition, Authority, Challenges
Avoids	Rejection, Intimacy, Relationships, Relaxation
Ability	Follow-Through, Vision, Tenacity, Reliability

When relating with a **SQUARE:**

- Be accurate, focused, and direct.
- Allow them to guide the conversation.
- Be respectful of their time.

Areas of contention and frustration:

- Questioning their authority or decisions.
- Being late and disorganized.
- Getting off topic.

ORGANIZED TRIANGLE

Strengths	Detailed, Loyal, Analytical, Intuitive
Weaknesses	Private, Negative, Fixating, Suspicious
Desires	Privacy, Perfection, Stability, Excellence
Avoids	Conversation, Failure, Compromise, Chaos
Ability	Organization, Creativity, Empathy

When relating with a **TRIANGLE:**
- Be prepared and stay focused.
- Give them room to be creative.
- Respect their personal space.

Areas of contention and frustration:
- Talking too much and too loud.
- Being sloppy or informal.
- Upsetting their system of organization.

OBSERVANT OCTAGON

Strengths	Patient, Listener, Tolerant, Dry Wit
Weaknesses	Worry, Fear, Laziness, Shy, Saying No
Desires	Peace, Humor, Support, Resolution
Avoids	Decisions, Deadlines, Negativity, Confrontation
Ability	Consistent, Calm, Loyal, Objective, Sensitive

- When relating with an **OCTAGON:**
- Be patient and positive.
- Be calm and do not rush.

Areas of contention and frustration:

- Requiring decisions on the spot.

- Instigating confrontation.

- Being dishonest or disguising your intentions.

The beauty of discovering your temperament is that you begin to understand why you act and react the way you do. I don't believe it gives you permission to justify your behavior, but it does allow you to understand your behavior and work to develop it to your best advantage. You have God-given strengths and weaknesses that make you who you are, and as you walk with Him, He will bring out the best in you—"He will refine you like silver and test you like gold" *(Zechariah 13:9, NIV)*.

OUR **RELATIONSHIP** WITH GOD

One of the most fulfilling aspects of our identity is found in our relationship with Christ. This doesn't mean that people who don't know Christ don't have identities, but the presence or absence of Christ in our lives shapes who we are and how we think, feel, and behave. Those who lack intimacy with the Father are more prone to feeling incomplete and to questioning who they are and what their purpose is in life. This is God's design: He has made us to need Him, and we are only our best when we are living in Him.

As we learned in the previous chapter, God's opinion of us is the only one that truly matters. He has called us into being and created us just the way He wants us, from the experiences He's led us through to the strengths and weaknesses of our personalities. He wants to show us that we are His beloved daughters and that He has a plan and purpose for each of us.

God had a clear plan and purpose for Deborah, a woman in the Bible who knew her God-given identity. The story is found in the Old Testament book of Judges. Deborah was the appointed judge for the people of Israel at that time. The Jewish nation was losing the war with Canaan and the people were full of fear and defeat. Deborah called for Barak, the commander-in-chief, to come meet with her about the situation they had found themselves in. As a spiritual leader in Israel, Deborah had seen it all, and she trusted in God to provide for His people. She spoke the word of the Lord to Barak, telling him to take ten thousand men to fight their oppressor, Sisera.

I'm sure Barak's response came as a surprise to Deborah. "If you will go with me, then I will go; but if you will not go with me, I won't go" *(Judges 4:8, NIV)*. Without missing a beat, Deborah responded with words of leadership and vision: "Certainly I will go with you, but because of the course you are taking, the honor will not be yours, for the Lord will deliver Sisera into the hands of a woman" *(4:9)*. Deborah foresaw Jael, another woman with a clear, God-given purpose and identity, defeating the enemy commander.

What I love about this story is that Deborah knew her identity. God had gifted, called, and equipped her to be the judge in Israel. She did not cower or retreat in her time of leadership. God designed her with a strong personality of leadership and led her to the experience of becoming a female judge over a patriarchal society; her relationship with Him and her security in her personality and experiences allowed her to lead Israel and effectively make the necessary decisions to win the battle.

When I met Kristen Dalton Wolfe, Miss USA 2009, I saw a woman who is secure in her God-given identity. She has created the "She Is More" ministry to show young women their royal identities as daughters of the One True King.[9] Here is her story about finding her identity:

I was raised in a Christian home, went to church every Sunday, and was actively involved in youth group, Bible study, and mission trips. As the oldest of four children, my definition for success was performance + approval. I never felt beautiful, I wasn't comfortable in my own skin. I dealt with painful cystic acne, loneliness, and depression. I believed if I could win Miss USA, I would finally feel worthy and beautiful and that all my insecurities would disappear.

In 2009, my childhood dream of winning Miss USA came true.

As incredibly exciting as it was, it wasn't the magical cure I thought it would be. I doubted myself all the time, I wanted to please everyone, and I spent many nights crying alone on the bathroom floor of my NYC titleholder apartment. I soon found that there is only emptiness in seeking the affirmation of a title or accolade to give me identity.

One day, someone spoke words to me that changed my life forever. I was doubting my purpose in life and my friend said to me, "Kristen, don't you know that you are a daughter of the One True King?" I had never heard or even thought of that before. But yes, he was right. This was a revelation and eye-opening—a complete paradigm shift to the way I had been seeing myself and living. This meant I was *royalty*. This meant I was His *Princess*. This meant I was born for royal purpose.

You are His Princess too—you have a royal identity that no title or worldly crown could ever give you and can never be taken away. When we accept Our King's hand and choose Him in return, our former nature and old ways melt away and transform into an everlasting royal identity that gives us a life with unshakable access to His power and confidence.

Kristen had been trying to find her identity in being Miss USA, but she was not seeing herself as a daughter of God and an heir to the kingdom of heaven. Once she found her identity in Christ, she found the true feelings of beauty and worth she had been longing for.

Understanding how our experiences have affected us and learning the shapes of our personalities is important. However, to understand our identities and to be at peace with who we are, we must recognize ourselves as daughters of the King. One thing I hope I have communicated through this book is that you are a unique individual with independent dreams, gifts, and goals. You are unique because God took the time to create you; He knows your strengths and weaknesses and has been beside you through life's journey. He has a plan and purpose that you will discern as you walk with Him. He has given you a beautiful identity that will blossom and flourish as you seek to know Him more.

COACHING EXERCISE

In this coaching exercise, spend some time thinking about the three aspects of your identity—your experiences, personality, and relationship with God. Be honest with yourself as you explore your strengths and weaknesses. Understanding and embracing your personal identity is key to becoming a Woman of Influence.

CAPITALIZE ON YOUR STRENGTHS

List the five top strengths you have identified from your Strengths table.

_____

_____

_____

_____

In what ways are you currently using these strengths?

_____

_____

_____

How can your strengths be maximized to their fullest potential?

_____

_____

_____

CURB YOUR WEAKNESSES

If you don't control your weaknesses, they will control you. An important piece of becoming a Woman of Influence is knowing how to take responsibility for yourself. When personal weaknesses began to control your life it is time to do something about it.

COACHING EXERCISE

Exercise Control
Say I have a problem with sarcasm or laziness. These are areas where I can exercise self-control. I have the choice to either allow these things to be part of my life, or I can discipline myself to be conscientious about how I respond to others and to be proactive about situations where I might be tempted to be lazy.

Learn to Delegate
If I'm not great with organization or people skills, I may want to consider delegating those tasks to someone else in some situations. If I am involved with a charity fundraiser and lack presentation skills, I should not be the one to make the pitch for funds. I might be better interacting with people one-on-one for the drive while someone else organizes the event and another gives the presentation.

Decide to Develop
It is so easy to say, "I'm not good at that" or "that's not my thing." But the truth is we all can grow and stretch in unexpected ways to become the women God has created us to be. When we make the decision to no longer allow our fear or skill to define us, we then step into the place of personal development.

List the top five weaknesses from your personality assessment that you feel are keeping you from your personal best. Next to each one determine whether you should *control, delegate,* or *develop* that weakness.

_____

_____

_____

_____

_____

DIGGING DEEPER

Now I would like you to dig a little deeper into your life. Write two to three sentences for each question to define your personal beliefs, convictions, and desires. This exercise has proven to be one of the most telling assessments you can do to know who you truly are. Take your time and think through each question—the more you write, the more you will understand your identity.

What is your family background, i.e., ethnicity, religion, values, or traditions?

_____

_____

_____

_____

What are your personal convictions regarding religion, politics, and family?

_____

_____

_____

_____

What are your personal interest and hobbies?

_____

_____

_____

_____

How much of a role does your faith in God play a part in your life?

_____

_____

_____

_____

What do you love about your experiences and personality?

_____

_____

_____

_____

If you could do one thing with your passion to make a difference in this world, what would it be?

_____

_____

_____

_____

Remember, **our identities**
are a combination of our experiences, personality,
and relationship with God,
so if our lives change, our identities **are not lost.**
We may need time to readjust
to the changes, but we are all individuals
with unique dreams, goals, and gifts,
and **God still has a plan** for each of us.

FOOTNOTES

9 For more about Kristen Dalton Wolfe and the She Is More ministry, visit her website at www.sheismore.com or read her book, *Rise Up, Princess: 60 Days to Revealing Your Royal Identity.*

CHAPTER NINE

DISCOVER YOUR DESTINY

destiny (noun): The inevitable or necessary fate to which a particular person or thing is destined; one's lot.

For we are his workmanship, created in Christ Jesus for good works, which God prepared beforehand, that we should walk in them. *Ephesians 2:10 (ESV)*

Destiny is more than a phrase or cliche: It's God's road map for your life. We often hear, "It was destined to happen." But destined by whom? God alone holds the steps of His children, and He has a distinct plan for you. He has been walking beside you through this book and is waiting to take you forward into your destiny as you become a Woman of Influence.

GOD'S **CALLING**

We see a beautiful example of God's calling and plan in the story of Esther. God's plan for this young girl was woven in time before she ever knew her name. Esther had lost her mother and father as a child and was under the guardianship of her cousin Mordecai. She was among the Jews who had been deported from Jerusalem and were now living in a foreign land. When the king decided it was time for a new queen, all the young maidens were called in for observation. Mordecai warned Esther to hide her nationality and family background, for a Jew would not have been a contestant for the court. It took a whole year of preparation just to be seen by the king, but Esther was highly loved and favored by everyone she met and was soon elevated to the king's court. Once the king saw Esther, it was all over. She was to be his queen.

Even when Esther began to live as a queen, she still made time to meet with Mordecai. She knew her identity was that of a Jew and she respected her culture. Her time as queen was from the hand of God and she knew it came with a cost. God had given her beauty and skill for a purpose, and she was prepared to fulfill her destiny. When the king's right-hand man advised him to rid the country of the Jews, Mordecai went to Esther, urging her to use her influence to speak to the king; he saw that God had placed her in the court "for such a time as this" *(Esther 4:14, NIV)*.

With boldness and confidence Esther approached the king's court, knowing it could cost her very life. As she paused to be summoned by the king, I'm sure her mind raced with thoughts of purpose and destiny. This is indeed what cousin Mordecai meant when he told her God had a plan for her life. What a beautiful picture of a women's destiny we see in Esther as the king lifted his scepter for the queen to enter.

Like Esther, we, too, have been summoned by God to enter our eternal destiny. You may be thinking to yourself, *I can't even think about what to make for dinner, let alone my eternal destiny,* but that is the beauty of this story. God had it all planned before Esther was crowned queen, and He has it all planned for you as well.

My good friend, Tiffany Dupont, played the role of Esther in the motion picture *One Night with the King* (2006). She is a beautiful actress with talent and charisma. But her greatest gift is her passion. You see, Tiffany knew at a young age what her destiny was—to use her talents as a platform for speaking to and encouraging women. Here's her story in her own words:

> My father, John Dupont, likes to tell the story of how I always knew what I wanted to be when I grew up. He claims that I knew, literally, since the day I was born. That particular day, my birthday, was a good three weeks past my original due date, and at the time, it appeared I was still rather inclined to stay put. So the doctor induced labor around lunchtime the following day, and I arrived swiftly in less than three hours. After the nurse swaddled me up and passed me to my dad, he noticed I was staring at something rather intensely for a baby only a few hours old. He could barely distract me as I seemed laser beamed to something behind him in the room. This was very odd, as it is incredibly difficult for newborns to hold their focus on anything for

more than a few moments. However, I remained focused. He looked over his shoulder to see what I was so fixated on, and sure enough, there it was, a television propped up in the corner behind him.

John Dupont will tell you, since the day I was born, I knew my destiny. I knew I'd be on that TV. I knew I wanted to be an actress, and it's true, I haven't wavered since. As I grew up, my inherent strengths and talent naturally bent towards a career in entertainment. I worked hard, stayed focused, and opportunities to build my career as an actress opened up all around me. My work and dedication has made me into a strong woman of depth, not void of bruises and woes, or of loneliness and doubt, but one striving hard to bring a weighted perspective to what can often be a very sugary, superficial arena. Being in the public eye, playing dress-up and make-believe for a living, it can all begin to feel like working towards buying the most exquisite Chanel bag only to discover it's just a knock-off filled with fluff. So much of my industry focuses on the exterior fanfare of material highs, things that were never the draw for me. So what is it all for, if the fleeting feeling of entertaining an audience and receiving superficial accolades aren't my incentives?

Love. Always.

That's my incentive, my motivator. Connecting that love to the largest audience possible is my goal. I have always distinctly known and felt that I have so much to give. That somehow my heart was filled with far more than I knew what to do with. That my life's purpose is charged with the responsibility to shepherd all that I have been given. I work as hard as I do in order to have the farthest reach, knowing that my purpose—my destiny—is to share what I've been given with as many people as possible. One of the many ways I get to do that is not only through acting but also through the numerous opportunities acting brings to my life. I've been granted the chance to mentor younger women, work with teen girls who have come from neglect and abuse, and share my story through public speaking to encourage unity within the female community. Being granted innate confidence, a distinctive presence, and a natural unabashed joy for life has propelled me on the very path I live out today.

GOD'S TIMING

God's timing is perfect. He knows our dreams and aspirations and has a clear plan of getting us there. Sometimes His timing is not what we anticipate or hope for—just imagine being Esther and having to wait a whole year just to have a king decide whether or not she was pretty enough for him! But God is outside of time, and He knows all that is going to happen. You may not be able to see right now why you are stuck in a job you hate or when you will find the perfect partner or start a family, but God sees your destiny and is leading you there.

Elizabeth, the mother of John the Baptist, is a fantastic example of a woman who had a destiny that God revealed in His own perfect time. When the story opens, we find that she and her husband Zechariah were a Godly couple who had no children: "Both of them were upright in the sight of God, observing all the Lord's commandments and regulations blamelessly. But they had no children, because Elizabeth was barren; and they were both well along in years" *(Luke 1:6-7, NIV)*.

Elizabeth was growing older and her desire for a child was closing in on her. I'm sure she had reasoned many times, *God, why me?* Being barren for any woman can be heartbreaking, but in that time, others would have seen her barrenness as a curse from God. I'm sure Elizabeth and Zechariah had often prayed together and discussed their problem getting pregnant, but after so many years without a child, reasoned it was just not meant to be.

When the angel of the Lord appeared to Zechariah one day in the temple, he was reasonably startled. Angels weren't in the habit of showing up those days; the Scripture's last mention of an angel appearing to someone was to Daniel, over 500 years earlier. The angel said to him, "Do not be afraid, Zechariah; your prayer has been heard. Your wife Elizabeth will bear you a son, and you are to give him the name John. He will be a joy and delight to you, and many will rejoice because of his birth" *(Luke 1:14-15, NIV)*.

I love the humor of the Bible. When Zechariah questioned God (I can relate for sure), the angel told him that because he doubted the promise of God, "You will now be silent and not able to speak until the day this happens, because you did not believe my words, which will come true at their proper time" *(Luke 1:19-20, NIV)*. Zechariah came out of the temple, but he couldn't tell anyone what had happened! So he high-tailed it home to Elizabeth, and the next thing we hear, she is pregnant (which didn't require any talking). When Elizabeth conceived, she stayed at home for five months, saying, "The Lord has done this for me… in these days He has shown his favor and taken away my disgrace among the people" *(Luke 1:25, NIV)*.

God had a destiny in mind for his daughter Elizabeth. While she hoped for children in her youth, He had his own timing and plan—timing that could not be any different for a son who was to be the forerunner of the Messiah. Her son, John the Baptist, was the earthly cousin of Jesus and the prophesied one who would prepare the way for the Lord (Isaiah 40:3-5).

Our destiny is before us, and God has a reason for the way in which it unfolds. Step by step, the Father of mankind prepares our way into His perfect plan for us. So often we get sidetracked or set back by circumstances and disappointments. We need to trust that our destiny is in the hands of a loving and all-powerful Father God who has a reason for each direction the journey takes us on.

When I once felt overwhelmed by a setback, my son Josh said to me, "Mom, keep your eye on where you're going, not on what's going on." Those words have kept me going more times then he will ever know.

I recently found a journal from 1999 that I had stuck away on my top shelf. As I sat down and read my thoughts, one page took me by surprise. The date was Sunday, March 22, 1999. It had been a season of reflection and spiritual contemplation for me. My heart was seeking and searching for the depths of God in a very intimate way. Each morning I would awake and seek God for His revelation in my life. I was so desirous of being in the Spirit of God and doing His will.

On that Sunday morning in March 1999, I'd written these words: *If I could design the perfect ministry for me, what would it look like?* I went on to list the items I would like to see God doing in my life. I wrote things I would like to accomplish as well as ministries I would like to begin. My list was very specific:

- I would like to teach and lead a large women's group.
- I would like to organize the ministry in a way to reach all women.

- I would like to take Jennie with me to speak.
- I want to travel to third-world countries.
- I want to teach women to understand their worth.
- I want to speak on large platforms.
- I want to mobilize women and resources for the ministry.

I believe that because I voiced my dreams and believed that God had equipped me for the task, it truly became my destiny. I knew what I wanted to do and I took actions to do it. Looking back on that journal now fourteen years later, I realize I have done everything on my list. When you place a dream on paper and ask God to use you for His Kingdom, get ready for great things to happen.

A RECIPE FOR DESTINY

Your experiences, abilities, desires, and opportunities are all woven together to make the predestined plan of God. A Woman of Influence looks ahead to her destiny, keeping in mind that God's perfect plan will be accomplished in His time. To prepare yourself for your journey, consider the following list that will guide your thoughts and actions along the way. Let's look at the recipe for destiny:

Dreams- what you want to do

Events- opportunities that come your way

Spiritual Gifts- God-given traits that are supernatural

Thoughts- a positive mindset and belief in the outcome

Interest- things you are attracted to

Niche- abilities that you uniquely possess

Yield- trusting that God is in control of your future

"I am on my way to becoming the **woman God** sees me to be."

COACHING EXERCISE

WRITING OUT MY DESTINY

Now it's time for you to write your destiny before the Lord. Using the recipe for destiny answer the following questions.

Dreams – What you want to do

If you could look five years down the road what would your life look like? This can include family, career, dreams, accomplishments, opportunities, relationships, etc. Write everything you dream for your future. Remember, if you can't see it, you won't receive it.

_____

_____

_____

_____

_____

_____

Events – Opportunities that come your way

What events would you like to see happen in your life? Think of these as opportunities that come your way. They can be in the form of business ventures, ministries, leadership responsibilities, event planning, etc. How has God wired you to lead? What would you like to be organizing or leading five years from today?

_____

_____

_____

_____

_____

Spiritual Gifts – God-given traits that are supernatural

We all have a spiritual gift. Use the passages in I Corinthians 12: 4-11 and Romans 12:6-8 for a listing of spiritual gifts and ask yourself what gift comes most naturally to you? What do others say you do well? If you could use your gift in a specific way in the future, what would that look like?

_____

_____

_____

_____

_____

_____

Thoughts – A positive mindset and belief in the outcome

Thoughts play a huge role in the outcome of your destiny. Our minds will try to convince us that we are not capable or equipped for a certain task or role. Your biggest battle is not your ability; it is your mindset. Once again the Bible is clear with God's plan for your mind. It tells us in *Proverbs 23:7*, "For as he thinks in his heart, so is he" (NKJV). Your thoughts will dictate your destiny. I have a saying that I rehearse daily to keep me focused on God's plan for my life. It goes like this: "I am on my way to becoming the woman God sees me to be." I say that over and over to myself when obstacles and setbacks come my way. My mind can be the greatest asset to my destiny or the biggest deterrent, depending on how I choose to use it. God tells us in *I Corinthians 2:16*, "But we have the mind of Christ." What do you think God has in mind for you? How will you remind yourself to be positive?

_____

_____

_____

_____

_____

_____

Interest – Things you are attracted to

I love this ingredient in the recipe for destiny because it is what excites me. If I were to ask you what your interests are, what would you say? They could be anything from working with kids, helping the homeless, writing music, designing clothes, creating websites—the list goes on and on. What is so beautiful about this element is that it has your name written all over it. Your destiny will always be in an area in which you have a natural interest. Make a list of five things you love to do.

_____

_____

_____

_____

Niche – Abilities that you uniquely possess

We all have abilities that just come naturally to us. My daughter was born to communicate. After she graduated from college she asked her daddy what he thought she should do for a living. He responded with one word. Talk! She is a natural when it comes to talking. She has the ability to hear what is being said and respond with great wisdom and passion. That is just a gift that comes naturally to her, but is not so with everyone. I've heard that next to death, the second most feared thing to do is public speaking, so when you speak in a crowd with complete confidence, that is a true niche in life. What is your niche? What ability do you uniquely possess? List five things that you believe to be your natural niche.

_____

_____

_____

Yield – Trusting that God is in control of your future

Ultimately your destiny is in the hands of God. His timing and molding come by yielding yourself to His perfect plan. I don't believe my destiny is a matter of fate, but faith. I believe as I act on the recipe for destiny, I will see the realization of what God had planned for me all along. God instructs us in His word to ask, seek, and knock for the things we want in our life. What can you do to remind yourself to yield to God's control?

_____

_____

_____

_____

_____

Ask and it will be given to you; seek and you will find; knock and the door will be opened to you. *Matthew 7:7 (NIV)*

As you write out your recipe for destiny, I believe that you, like me, will one day look back on your responses and see God has answered your request.

DEVELOP A STRATEGIC SYNERGY

In the previous chapters, you have discovered and defined the significance of your Life Map and the shape of your identity, so it is time to consider what that means for your future. Strategic Synergy is developing a plan with purpose and intention, utilizing the knowledge you have gained, along with your unique abilities, to create the best opportunity for personal success. With the insights you have gleaned from the combination of the last two chapters, the Strategic Synergy process will assist you in developing a clear plan that will keep you focused and confident you are on the right path to becoming a Woman of Influence.

What are the three words you identified while doing your Life Map that best describe you?

_____

_____

_____

_____

What are the top three strengths you discovered in your Personality Assessment?

_____

_____

_____

_____

What are the top three weaknesses you discovered in your Personality Assessment?

_____

_____

_____

_____

List three things you would like to accomplish in the next year.

For example, learn a new language, run a marathon, go back to school, start a business, build a relationship, change jobs.

_____

_____

_____

_____

Now using the words that best define you, along with your personal strengths while avoiding your weaknesses, take one of the above goals and write three steps you are willing to take to create a plan of action.

_____

_____

_____

_____

Your destiny is in God's hands. A Woman of Influence knows her destiny and is daily walking towards it, making the most of her opportunities.

When you place a **dream**
on paper and **ask God** to use you
for His Kingdom, get ready for
great things to happen.

CONCLUSION

Congratulations on your journey to becoming a Woman of Influence. What a privilege to walk with you through this exciting process! Most women don't take the time necessary to get to know just who they really are. The process can seem overwhelming and intimidating, but you have taken the first steps by completing the exercises in this book. Whether you are still trying to skip over obstacles or are taking a jump into your future, you are on your way to a great start.

My prayer for you is that you will never stop playing hopscotch. I pray that the sense of adventure and intrigue will be your lifelong companions and that you will always aspire to use your influence to touch others for the good of humanity. I pray that God's goodness and favor will travel with you and that you may be a light to those who call you friend.

I want to encourage you to never stop growing. The assessments in this book can be done over and over again. Set big goals and see God's dreams. This is just the beginning of your life of Influence; you are destined to affect the lives of those around you. Not long ago, I was walking toward a group of ladies and noticed they were all laughing. "What is so funny?" I asked. "You," they replied. They then explained how my belief in them had stretched, pulled, challenged, and promoted them to greatness. They said I saw them as Women of Influence way before they did. That is what being a Woman of Influence is about—seeing the best in others and helping them get there.

I want to extend an invitation for you to join me at our annual Women of Influence Conference. You can also follow Women of Influence through social media for inspiration and encouragement. Facebook, Twitter, Instagram, blogs, and our website are great ways to stay in touch and share experiences.

Blessings and Abundance,

Tammy Hotsenpiller

76958782R00106

Made in the USA
San Bernardino, CA
17 May 2018